The Wines of Portugal

The Wines of
PORTUGAL

JAN READ

faber and faber

First published in 1982
by Faber and Faber Limited
3 Queen Square, London WC1N 3AU
Filmset by Latimer Trend & Company Ltd Plymouth
Printed in Great Britain by
Ebenezer Baylis & Son Ltd
The Trinity Press, Worcester
All rights reserved

British Library Cataloguing in Publication Data

Read, Jan
The wines of Portugal
1. Wine and wine making—Portugal
I. Title
641.2′2′09469   TP559.P/

ISBN 0–571–11951–4
ISBN 0–571–11952–2 Pbk

Library of Congress Cataloging in Publication Data

Read, Jan
The wines of Portugal

Bibliography: p.
Includes index.
1. Wine and wine making—Portugal. I. Title.
TP559.P8R4 1982   641.2′22′0946   82–7313
ISBN 0–571–11951–4   AACR2
ISBN 0–571–11952–2 (pbk.)

FOR LUÍS CHARTERS, WHOSE ENERGY AND
ENTHUSIASM HAVE DONE SO MUCH TO
AROUSE A WIDER INTEREST IN THE
WINES OF HIS NATIVE PORTUGAL

Contents

CONTENTS

10

Illustrations

COLOUR

MONOCHROME

MAPS

Acknowledgements

Anyone who writes about wine must know how impossible it would be to put together a reliable book without regular access to tastings and visits to the vineyards and wineries.

Beginning, as does the wine, with its making, I should first of all like to thank D. Luís Charters of the Portuguese Government Trade Office in London for arranging frequent visits to the different wine-producing areas of the country. His colleagues of the Fundo de Fomento de Exportação in Lisbon, D. João Renano Henriques, Dna. Eva Maria Blovsky and Dna. Maria Helena Gomes Martins, went to great trouble to organize the complicated journeyings from one end of Portugal to the other. In the field, the representatives of the official regulatory bodies, such as the Comissão da Região dos Vinhos Verdes and the Federação dos Vinicultores do Dão, were most helpful, and I am especially grateful to D. Amândio Barbedo Galhano of the Comissão for his advice on technical matters and to its Chief of Public Relations, D. Fernando Nuno Gaspar, who gave up so much time to driving my wife and myself around the byroads of the Minho.

The wine-makers themselves were always free with their information and generous with their hospitality. Of those whom we visited on recent occasions, I should particularly like to thank an old friend, D. Fernando van-Zeller Guedes of SOGRAPE and his nephews, D. Luís and D. Antonio van-Zeller Guedes of the Sociedade Agrícola da Quinta da Aveleda. D. Fernando Porto Soares Franco, his son António and D. Jorge de Avillez of José Maria da Fonseca Succrs. are always the most welcoming of hosts, and I am under a special obligation to both SOGRAPE and J. M. da Fonseca for contributing towards the cost of illustrating the

15

book. The Bairrada Wine Growers Association has also made a generous contribution.

Among friends in Oporto who have been of great assistance are D. Jorge Ferreira and D. Fernando Moreira Paes Nicolau de Almeida of A. A. Ferreira Succrs. and Mr. David Delaforce of Delaforce Sons and Ca. The other wine-makers who both opened their *adegas* to us and most generously entertained us are too numerous to mention, but it would be churlish not to thank D. José Rodrigues Sampaio of the Vinícola do Vale do Dão; D. Luís Costa of Caves São João; D. Mário Briosa Neves of Caves Aliança; D. Idelberto Soares of Caves Velhas; D. Ricardo Nicolau de Almeida of Borges & Irmão; D. Julio de Almeida Machado of Carvalho, Ribeiro & Ferreira; D. António Bernardino Paulo da Silva of Vinhos Beira-Mar; D. A de Castro e Sousa of the Quinta das Bouças; and D. Vasco Neiva Correia of the cooperative at Torres Vedras.

By way of tastings and supplying samples, the British agents of the firms have also been of major assistance, among them D. Jorge Gonçalves Dias of Atkinson, Baldwin Ltd; D. Fausto Ferraz and D. Dino Ventura of D. & F. Wines Ltd; Mr. P. C. Conway of Winckleton Ltd; Mr. G. S. R. Maggs of Adega Wines Ltd; Miss Sheila Vere Nicoll of Caxton Wines Ltd; Mr. John Rawlings of Rawlings, Voigt Ltd; Mr. David Cossart of Cossart, Gordon & Co. Ltd; and Mr. D. V. B. Pamment of Blayney & Co., Sunderland.

I am grateful to my publishers, Messrs. Faber & Faber Ltd, for leave to reproduce the plate from the late Mr. H. Warner Allen's *History of Wine*; to Mr. Hugh Johnson for tasting a range of white Buçaco wines on my behalf; to Mr. Peter Lewis of the Wine & Spirit Association of Great Britain for guidance on labelling and EEC regulations; and to my editor, Mr. Julian Jeffs for his advice and encouragement. My wife, Maite Manjón, has kindly contributed the chapter on 'Food with Wine', and without her help as interpreter on our travels I should have been lost indeed!

Foreword

Port, as befits its reputation, has been well served by writers and historians of wine. Beginning with accounts such as John Croft's famous *Treatise on the Wines of Portugal* of 1788 and J. J. Forrester's *Oliveira Prize-Essay on Portugal* of 1853, its growth pangs and evolution have been described at length; and more recently a succession of well-informed writers—H. Warner Allen, Rupert Croft-Cooke, André Simon, Sarah Bradford, George Robertson and Wyndham Fletcher to name only some—have taken the story up to the present day.

In regard to table wines, matters are very different. Until Raymond Postgate published his slender volume on *Portuguese Wine* in 1969, very little, and nothing of much substance, was available to the English-speaking reader—and, though it remains an elegant and intuitive essay, the production and export of the wines have since changed out of all recognition.

The reason for this hiatus is simple. The wine scene in Portugal was for so long dominated by Port—and to a lesser extent by Madeira—that the Portuguese were late in developing their beverage wines and in demarcating the better growths. The *vinhos verdes* are at last being shipped in large amount and drunk with enjoyment abroad; the sparkling rosés have for long been enormously popular; and it will be surprising if the wines from regions such as the Dão and Bairrada do not repeat their success. It therefore seems an opportune moment to revise and split up my *Wines of Spain and Portugal* and to devote a separate book to wines which so richly repay more detailed study.

17

SPAIN

Minho
Monçao
Viana do
Castelo
Barcelos
Braga
Bragança
Penafiel
PORTO
Douro
Vila Real
Régua
2
Lamego
Pinhel
Aveiro
Viséu
PINHEL
SPAIN
4
3
Dão
Mondego
Figueira
da Foz
Coimbra

Castel Branco

Tejo
Obidos
Santarem
RIBATEJO
TORRES
VEDRAS
Elvas
Sintra
6
Estremoz
5
LISBOA
7
8
Evora
A
L
E
N
T
E
J
O
Guadiana
Beja

9
Lagoa
Faro

Demarcated regions:

1 Vinhos Verdes
2 Port
3 Dão
4 Bairrada
5 Colares
6 Bucelas
7 Carcavelos
8 Setúbal
9 Algarve

Undemarcated region:
PINHEL

Production greater than 50
hectolitres per square kilometre

0   50   100 km

The wine-growing areas of Portugal

Historical Introduction

The early history of Portugal is that of the Iberian Peninsula as a whole, since it was not until the twelfth century that an independent kingdom was established; and for this reason the first stages in viticulture closely resemble the pattern in Spain. Reviewing the matter in his *Landscapes of Bacchus*, a scholarly volume devoted to the interplay between the culture of the vine and the geography and economic history of Portugal, Professor Dan Stanislawski considers it likely that

> Some five thousand years ago the Almerians of southern Spain were gathering grapes, and probably the early central European migrants, who arrived in north-west Iberia at the end of the second millennium BC, would have followed the practices of their relatives of the Alpine and northern forests of prehistoric times: gathering the edible, sweet fruits and, possibly pressing them to make wine.

As in Spain, it is likely that the vine was first properly domesticated by the Phoenicians; and viticulture was further extended and developed by the later Greek and Roman colonists. Concrete evidence of Roman wine-making procedures has been found in the shape of *dolia*, closely resembling the *tinajas* still in use in La Mancha and southern Spain and also in parts of the Portuguese Alentejo, where they are known as *tarefas de barro*. In the first century BC, Strabo describes the culture of the vine among the Lusitanians on the western coasts of Iberia and further reports that it was spreading into the mountains of the north-west. The Portuguese are conservative in their techniques of farming, and the high-growing vine, so prevalent in the north of the country today, is probably a Roman survival.

19

Lusitania, like the other Roman provinces of Iberia, was overrun successively by the Visigoths and the Moors; but it seems that here, as elsewhere in the Peninsula, the Moslems were reluctant to enforce the Koran's injunction against wine. It is on record that Lorvão, a Christian monastery near Coimbra, cultivated its vines throughout the Moorish domination; and vineyards were widespread throughout the southern and central areas of the Alentejo, the Portuguese Estremadura and Beira Central.

It is something of a puzzle why, towards the end of this period and at the time of the Reconquest of the country by the Christians, vineyards should have disappeared from southern Portugal, never to be fully restored. The most likely explanation is that widespread famine followed the fighting and that the land was either employed for growing wheat and olives or given over to hunting preserves for the kings and nobles.

It was at this same period, when Alfonso VI of Castile was making inroads into Moorish al-Andalus, that the Kingdom of Portugal took shape. Its first independent king, Afonso Henriques, took up the struggle and his successors fought a war on two fronts, against the Moors and their Spanish neighbours. Portugal reached its present boundaries when Afonso III (1248–79) finally expelled the Moors from the Algarve and consolidated his position by marrying the daughter of Alfonso X of León and Castile. Even after the decisive defeat of the Castilians at Aljubarrota in 1385 by the combined forces of Portugal and England, Spain continued to cast covetous eyes on her smaller neighbour. She suffered a further period of Spanish domination at the hands of Philip II, and it was not until the Restoration of 1640 and the founding of the Bragança dynasty that the country was at last secure.

England has always been the traditional ally of Portugal in war and her trading partner in peace. In 1373, following a damaging attack on Lisbon by Henry II of Castile, Edward III signed an agreement pledging friendship between the two countries. The English alliance, confirmed by the Treaty of Windsor in 1386, was often renewed; and more than six hundred years later, Portugal is still Britain's oldest ally.

In early times Portugal traded sea-salt, oranges, hides, cork and, of course, wine, in exchange for English woollens and salt cod—still, in the form of *bacalhau*, a staple of the diet. After

20

the epic voyages of discovery of Prince Henry the Navigator (1394–1460) and Portugal's emergence as the leading sea-faring nation of the time, the range of trading commodities was expanded to include tropical products and spices from Africa, the East and Brazil.

It appears that the first import of Portuguese wines into England began in the twelfth century. There is some doubt as to the character and origin of the legendary 'Osey', but it was probably an unsweetened natural wine. The name has been derived from the French *oseille* (or sorrel) and from Auxerre, at one time supposed to be the place of its origin. André Simon to all purposes clinched the matter by discovering a manuscript which described Osey as an *alternative* to Auxerre. He also unearthed an early English poem containing the lines:

Portyngalers . . .
Whose merchandise cometh much into England.
Their land hath oil, wine, osey, wax and grain.

Although the claims of Setúbal, rather south of the capital, have been advanced by Professor Stanislawski and others (see p. 71),

Winemaking as depicted by eighteenth-century azulejos *in the Casa Anadia at Mangualde in the Dão. (Jan Read)*

21

the wine may well have come from further north, since Lisbon was in the hands of the Moors until 1147.

Until 1453 the English Customs levied a uniform tunnage duty on all wines, but thereafter the excise on beverage wines was fixed at 3 shillings a tun, and that for sweet dessert wines at 6 shillings. Since at the time there was no scientific way of establishing alcoholic degree, the authorities resorted to the simple expedient of lumping in the Portuguese wines with other fortified wines from the Peninsula, such as the popular sack from Jerez. This was to prove an increasing handicap for the exporters of Portuguese table wines, and after 1557 very little more was heard of Osey in England.

The other famous Portuguese wine of the early period was Charneco, mentioned several times in English literature of the late sixteenth and early seventeenth centuries. In Act II, scene 3 of *Henry VI*, Part II, of 1594, Shakespeare describes a duel between Horner the Armourer and his apprentice, Peter. The over-confident Horner fortified himself with a cup of sack, another of Charneco and a 'pot of good double beer'—and was promptly struck down by his neophyte assistant. Thanks to the discriminatory excise regulations, which put the Portuguese wines at a disadvantage *vis à vis* those from Gascony, Charneco, too, disappeared. H. Warner Allen went to considerable trouble to identify its place of origin and finally discovered that one of the sub-districts of Bucelas (see p. 64), just north of Lisbon, is named Charneca, and therefore came to the conclusion that Charneco was a Bucelas wine.

By the late seventeenth century, the situation had materially changed. On the one hand, the lucrative trade in Lisbon sugar from Brazil had been undercut by exports from the new British colonies in the West Indies, and exporters in Portugal found themselves in desperate plight; on the other, after the marriage of William of Orange and Mary, deteriorating relations with France had led to retaliatory duties on French wines, so that by 1672 the normal 20,000 tuns of French wine imported into England had been cut down to 7500. The opportunity for increased exports of Portuguese wine was wide open, but the difficulty was to find anything of sufficient quality.

The merchants first looked to the Minho in the far north; British traders settled at the port of Viana do Castelo and a Vice-

Consulate was later opened there. The wines were plentiful and cheap, but then, as now, the vines grew high up trees and trellises, producing a light, acidulous wine with a marked bubble or *pétillance* (see Chapter 5). The technical problems of bottling and shipping the 'green wines' have now been overcome, but at the time, when they were shipped in cask, they often turned to vinegar before they could be sold. As late as 1704 English coopers were sent to the Minho in an effort to improve matters, and H. Warner Allen quotes from a letter written by Thomas Woodmass, the son of a Kettering wine merchant who served his apprenticeship at Viana: 'Ye English cupers are a drunken lot, but ye natives now know how to make casks.'

The wines achieved a limited success; but supplies were short, and the English taste was in any case for more full-blooded red wine. It was thus that the shippers turned their attention to the undeveloped Douro valley further south. In view of the state of viticulture and oenology at the period, it is hard to say why they should have supposed that its barren soils would produce the type of wine they so needed. In the event, the Douro grapes, because of the beating summer sunshine, proved to be exceptionally high in sugar and the problem turned out to be quite otherwise. Under the hot sun and in the primitive stone *lagares* used for making the wine, fermentation proceeded so fast and furiously that most of the flavour bubbled away and not a trace of sugar was left to soften it.

It was at this juncture that the producers and shippers stumblingly hit on the expedient of brandying the wine, so checking the final stages of fermentation—but this is the beginning of the story of Port, which deserves more detailed treatment of its own (pp. 39–42).

On the political front, with the outbreak of the War of the Spanish Succession in 1702, relations between France and Britain were finally ruptured. In the wake of a military treaty guaranteeing Portugal against foreign invasion, the more famous Methuen Treaty of 1703, formally establishing tariff preferences for Portuguese wines over French, was concluded between the two countries. Although the Portuguese, with brief interruptions, had enjoyed tariff preferences for a long time, the Methuen Treaty resulted in greatly increased exports of Port to England, for, as H. Warner Allen put it so well: 'It gave growers and shippers a promise of security in the British market without which they might well have despaired of success and abandoned the long expensive series of experiments which culminated so gloriously.'

There was one advance during the long development of Port which deserves mention here, since it had a profound effect on the making of fine wines everywhere. This was the introduction of the first cylindrical bottles, which thereafter made possible the prolonged ageing of wines in glass. Prior to about 1770, the bottles in use, both in Portugal and elsewhere, were squat in shape and were necessarily stored upright. The use of corks, common in the ancient world but later discontinued, had long since been rediscovered and put to good use by Dom Pérignon in making Champagne; but a cork out of contact with liquid soon shrinks and becomes porous, and the air space below is a breeding ground for harmful organisms that filter through. The new idea of binning bottles on their side to provide a liquid seal, in combination with corks of excellent quality made from the bark of the cork oaks so plentiful in Portugal (see also Chapter 12), made possible first the creation of vintage Port and later the splendid French vintage wines of the nineteenth century, after the new form of bottle had been introduced to Bordeaux from Portugal. The evolution of the Port bottle, exemplified by examples in the possession of Messrs. Berry Bros., Rudd and Company, is illustrated in the plate from H. Warner Allen's *A History of Wine*. It will be seen that there are considerable variations in the length of neck, but that the first bottle suitable for binning on its side is that of 1770.

Because of the overwhelming importance of Port in export markets (and, to a lesser degree, of Madeira, for which the largest outlet was traditionally the United States), for the next century and a half Portuguese table wines were produced almost entirely for home consumption and in small peasant *adegas*. It is true that the white wines of Carcavelos and Bucelas, grown in small regions near Lisbon, achieved a certain vogue among the officers of Wellington's army at the time of the Peninsular War and during the defence of the famous Lines of Torres Vedras, but the state of the industry may be gauged by extracts from the official catalogue listing the Portuguese entry at the London International Exhibition of 1874.

The Alentejo, the great tract to the south of Lisbon, is described as '*terra de mau pão e mau vinho*' ('a land of bad bread and bad

24

1708   1714   1719   1725

1739   1741   1753   1768

1770   1780   1793   1807   1812

The evolution of the Port bottle (from H. Warner, Allen, A History of Wine, *London, 1961)*

wine'), while of the Algarve the anonymous Portuguese compiler writes:

> It is proved that the wines of the Algarve, by its natural endowments, are not inferior to the wines of Madeira, Gerez and Málaga. In processes of vinification there is great careness and delaying.

However, our author qualifies this (and it seems a pity to amend his picturesque English) by continuing:

> Between samples there are defective wines. Damn was produced by careless and unskilfulness of productor . . . The drawing out from a great vessel a little quantity of wine is always a great danger to wine extracted. To this process it must very much attention and experience and cleanliness; when two thirds parts, at least, of Portuguese productors, which furnished samples, are entirely despisers of this matter.

As long ago as 1756, the Portuguese statesman and patriot, the Marquês de Pombal, as part of his measures for controlling abuses in the making of Port, had delimited the area in which the wine could be grown; but general improvement of the beverage wines did not take place until the government once again intervened during the first decade of the twentieth century. Largely on the insistence of the eminent oenologist, Professor Cincinnato da Costa, seven other regions were demarcated. It was from that time, and both because of technical advice from the bodies set up to control the regions and the construction of cooperatives where smallholders might take their grapes to be vinified, that wines such as the *vinhos verdes* and Dão underwent the steady improvement which has gained them a reputation far beyond their native Portugal.

Since the demarcation more than half a century ago of the original seven regions, other much larger wine-producing areas have become increasingly important, and the government's plans for further demarcation and regulation of the wine industry will be described in the next chapter. Another development over recent decades has been the enormous expansion in the production of sparkling rosé wines, such as 'Mateus' and 'Lancers', which have now outstripped Port both in volume and value of exports.

For such close neighbours, peopled by a common stock, Spain and Portugal are curiously detached—no doubt as a legacy of the feuding of the medieval period and Portugal's prolonged struggle for independence. The two countries have gone their own ways in making wine, though current developments in demarcating chosen areas and constructing networks of cooperative wineries are along broadly similar lines.

A striking difference is in methods of viticulture, particularly the Portuguese predilection for high-growing vines—in Spain, to be found only in Galicia. The reasons are both geographic and sociological. Spain is a large country with vast expanses of high plateau, parched for most of the year and particularly suited to low-growing vines in large unbroken expanses. Portugal, apart from a relatively narrow coastal strip, the Ribatejo north of Lisbon and the wide plains of the Alentejo to its south—now little used for growing grapes—is uniformly mountainous. Generally speaking, the level of the ground rises progressively from west to east, culminating in the high sierras of the Spanish border. The rain clouds from the Atlantic spend themselves against this natural 'amphitheatre'; and, apart from the summer months of June, July, August and September, the climate in the north, as in Galicia, tends to be wet and humid. There is therefore a positive advantage in training the vines well clear of the ground, so as to minimize rot and mildew.

The other reason for preserving the high vine—so alien to the well-ordered vineyards of France and on the face of it so archaic— is economic. Though Portugal possesses only one-fifth of the land area of Spain, her population amounts to one-third. As Professor Stanislawski well put it in *Landscapes of Bacchus*:

> Few places in the world support a more numerous rural population than does northwest Portugal. Anomalous in Portugal as a whole, this population is not concentrated in cities and towns but dispersed throughout the countryside on thousands of small properties cultivated with the devotion that is shown by gardeners.

By festooning the vines on the trees bordering his plot or by training them in arbours supported by tall granite pillars the Portuguese peasant in the north releases the rest of his land for food crops such as maize and the tall, dark green cabbage, or *couve*;

27

at the same time the vines provide a valuable wind-break to shelter the other crops.

The high-growing vine is typical of the main wine-producing areas of the north—though to judge from occasional examples from as far afield as Setúbal south of Lisbon, this form of cultivation is sometimes practised for decorative and traditional reasons. Again, in the high valley of the Douro, land economy takes the different form of steeply terraced hillsides planted with

Different modes of training the vine. (From Cyrus Redding, A History and Description of Modern Wines, *3rd ed., London, 1851)*

low-growing vines. These are also common in Galicia, but not elsewhere in Spain, except in isolated mountain areas such as the Priorato in Catalonia and the Maestrazgo inland from the Levante coast.

Portugal also differs from Spain—and this is one of the reasons why it is so unrewarding to compare the wines from the two countries—in that the industry has progressed from the era of the primitive peasant winery to that of the large-scale modern cooperative without the prior appearance of the numerous size-able private firms, so typical of a region like the Rioja. Although, for example, Dão is sold by private firms under a great variety of labels, the great bulk of the wine is produced in only ten cooperatives, from which the private concerns buy their wine ready-made to blend and mature it.

And here another factor comes into play. The Portuguese are strictly conservative about their wine, and after long centuries of fermenting the grapes, stalks and all, in open stone *lagares*, have acquired a taste for deep-coloured red wines high in alcohol, which to foreign consumers often seem unduly tannic and dry. Since until recently more or less the whole market was in Portugal and its dependencies, the cooperatives, although destalking the grapes, have tended to maintain this style by prolonged contact of the skins with the must; and when mellower, less astringent wines are required for export, they must perforce be aged for an extended period in oak. In a world where exports have become all-important, changes are on the way; but it is significant that the wines which have sold abroad in large amount are the white *vinhos verdes*, with their low degree of alcohol, and the light, sparkling rosés.

In hard figures, some 15 per cent of the population earns its living by making or selling wines, and the 350,000 hectares of vineyards give employment to some 235,000 rural workers during the year. There are about 180,000 individual wine-growers, most of them smallholders, since 87 per cent produce less than 100 hectolitres of wine, and 96 per cent less than 250 hectolitres. Between 35 and 40 per cent are members of the 113 cooperatives.

Portugal ranks sixth among the world's wine-producers with an average annual production over the last ten years of 10 million hectolitres. Internal consumption is of the order of 7.5 million hectolitres, and foreign shipments in 1980 amounted to 1,070,962 hectolitres of beverage wine and 614,502 hectolitres of Port, representing the country's largest single export.

Port has been known for so long as the world's most famous dessert wine that it needs no recommendation; but at a time when the fine table wines from France and elsewhere have risen so steeply in price, the many delicious growths from Portugal will amply repay study by wine-drinkers conscious both of price and quality.

1

Control and Labelling

As in most wine-growing countries, regulations controlling the production and sale of wine have existed in rudimentary form for a very long period. For example, in the Dão area, there are references to viticulture in some dozen documents dating between 1113 and 1146; and in 1242, the first of several such occasions, the citizens of Viseu petitioned the king to forbid the entry of wine into the area from outside while local supplies were available. There is also a long series of decrees relating to the production and sale of wines in Santarém and the surrounding region of the Ribatejo, beginning with a Royal Charter granted to the town by Afonso Henriques in 1170, followed by further decrees made by Pedro I in 1364, Fernando I in 1367, Afonso V (1438–81) and João II in 1467 and again in 1487.

The first thorough-going measures to control the making of a wine and to demarcate the area in which it might be produced were taken by the Marquês de Pombal in 1756, when he formed the Companhia Geral da Agricultura dos Vinhos do Alto Douro, better known as the Oporto Wine Company. His intention was to rectify abuses in the elaboration of port, such as its coloration with elderberry juice, and to curb the power of the British shippers, so ensuring the growers a decent return. Although the Upper Douro was officially demarcated a hundred years before the French took similar steps, Portugal was not, as is often stated, the first country to demarcate a wine-growing area. When I wrote something to this effect, I was promptly reminded by my friend David Peppercorn that the Grand Duke of Tuscany demarcated what is now the Chianti Classico region in 1716.

The 'Old Wine Company', having carried out numerous useful reforms before itself falling a victim to monopolistic abuse, had long ago disappeared from the scene when, in the wake of the Wall Street crash of 1929, various of the smaller Port firms failed and there was a crisis of overproduction. The government took stock of the situation and in June 1933 set up the present efficient system of control. It comprises three bodies: the Casa do Douro, supervising viticulture in the thousands of vineyards spread over the area; the Gremio dos Exportadores do Vinho do Porto (the Port Wine Shippers Association); and the Instituto do Vinho do Porto, controlling the other two organizations and charged with the overall supervision of the production and trading of Port. The work of these bodies will be described more fully in the next chapter.

For the reasons already explained, it was not until the early 1900s that the government took an active interest in the improvement of the wines from other regions, seven of which were then demarcated. These were:

Bucelas
Carcavelos
Colares
Moscatel de Setúbal
Vinhos Verdes
Dão
Madeira

To begin with, control of the different demarcated regions was vested in autonomous bodies, only two of which have survived, now known as the Comissão de Viticultura da Região dos Vinhos Verdes and the Federação dos Vinicultores do Dão. In 1937 a Junta Nacional do Vinho (JNV), with headquarters in Lisbon, was created by government decree to coordinate the activities of the different regulatory bodies for wines other than Port and to supervise production in the increasingly important undemarcated regions of the country. Its functions were subsequently extended by a long series of decrees issued both by the democratic republic and the Salazar dictatorship. In recent times the economic importance of the first four of the demarcated regions (Bucelas, Carcavelos, Colares and Moscatel de Setúbal), all of them tiny and near Lisbon, has declined—though they still produce some of Portugal's most individual wines. Their autonomous controlling organizations were therefore dissolved; and they, like Madeira and two newly demarcated regions, the Bairrada and Algarve, are now the direct responsibility of JNV.

On a larger scale, the powers and functions of the Junta Nacional resemble those of its smaller sister organizations, the Comissão in the Vinho Verde region and the Federação in the Dão, to be described in the chapters about the wines.

It compiles central statistics, keeps a register of vineyards and producers, authorizes grape varieties and methods of viticulture and vinification, and maintains analytical and research laboratories. JNV also extends technical assistance to the producers and provides storage facilities for surplus wine—and for this purpose

Seal affixed by the inspectorate of the Federação dos Vinicultores do Dão to a depósito in the cellars of Carvalho, Ribeiro and Ferreira near Lisbon.
(Jan Read)

The Douro valley, with its terraced port vineyards, near Pinhão. (Jan Read)

A barco rabelo *moored at the quay of Vila Nova de Gaia opposite Oporto. (Jan Read)*

The red roofs of the Port Lodges at Vila Nova de Gaia. (Jan Read)

the country is divided into a number of *zonas técnicas*. Another activity is the promotion of new cooperatives, for which it provides plans and arranges loans; and its technical advisers are, of course, always at the disposal of the local management committees. Further than this, the Junta organizes an annual Concurso Nacional de Vinhos Engarrafados, a nation-wide competition in which the producers of bottled wine from the different regions take part, and the prize-winners are awarded *Medalhas de Ouro* (gold medals), *Medalhas de Prata* (silver medals) and *Mencões Honrosas* (honourable mentions) on the recommendation of qualified juries. As an example of its efforts to publicize and promote Portuguese wines in general, it has recently produced and published an illustrated book, *Vinhos de nosso pais* ('The Wines of Our Country').

Last, and perhaps of most direct importance to the consumer, JNV authorizes the bottling of wine from the demarcated regions under its jurisdiction with a *selo de origem* ('seal of origin'), corresponding to the French Appellation d'Origine or Spanish Denominación de Origen. As in all the demarcated regions of Portugal, these seals take the form of a narrow, numbered paper strip, affixed to the cork and neck of the bottle before capsuling; they are issued to the producers in appropriate number only after the inspectorate is satisfied that the *adega* has produced the wine in accordance with its specifications. These include:

1. Boundaries of the region and sub-region.
2. Authorized types of wine.
3. Permitted varieties of grape and the proportions in which they may be used.
4. Maximum yield per hectare.
5. Traditional methods of vinification.
6. Period of ageing in cask and bottle, where applicable.
7. Analytical standards—degree of alcohol, specific gravity, content of fixed and volatile acid, etc.

Samples must be submitted to the Junta, and *selos de origem* are not authorized until the wine has passed analytical tests in its laboratories and has met with the approval of expert tasters.

It has long been recognized that there was a need for thoroughgoing reorganization of the system of demarcation, since, on the one hand, the importance of the small central regions has declined and, on the other, a number of other regions, widely scattered over the country, have now come into prominence and are making excellent wine in large amounts. Two of these regions, the Bairrada in the coastal area just south of Oporto, and the well-known holiday area of the Algarve in the far south, have very recently been demarcated.

Further than this, a Decree Law of 7 June 1979 and a Ministerial Order made in the following August, have established a new category of 'determinate areas' as a step towards full demarcation. The order defines these areas as follows:

2°–1 By 'determinate area' is understood an area or group of vinicultural areas producing wines with particular qualitative characteristics, where the name is used, as the case may be, to designate the wines or to indicate their origin.

2°–2 Regional names shall be used to designate the respective wines and must therefore stand out on the label of the bottled products when they refer to denominations linked with demarcated and regulated areas enjoying a statute of their own; and the expression 'demarcated area', or the equivalent in any other foreign language, may be added to those regional names.

3°–1 Vinicultural regions not yet demarcated and regulated by a statute of their own can enjoy the conditions of the previous articles only after a definition of their areas and other terms, taking into account the characteristics of their respective wines.

At the time of writing the 'determinate areas' recognized by the EEC Commission, additional to the Port region, the demarcated regions listed on page 31 and the sub-regions of the Vinhos Verdes (see pp. 89–95), are from north to south of the country:

Douro: Alijo, Lamego, Sabrosa, Vila Real
Beira Alta: Lafões, Meda
Estremadura: Torres Vedras, Palmela
Ribatejo: Cartaxo
Alentejo: Borba, Reguengos, Vidigueira.

In common with the demarcated growths, wines from any of these areas shipped to Community countries rank, in the legalistic jargon of the Commission, as equivalent to 'Quality Wines PSR' and are labelled accordingly:

MANDATORY INFORMATION

> Geographical unit
> Country of origin
> Name and address of bottler
> Name and address of importer (if bottled in Portugal)
> Nominal volume

PERMITTED INFORMATION

> Red—White—Rosé
> Smaller geographical unit
> Brand name
> Name and address of distributor
> Citation ('Established in . . .', etc.)
> Actual or total alcoholic strength
> Directions for serving
> Sweet/dry description
> History
> Vine variety
> Vintage
> Superior quality description
> Awards and medals
> Bottling on premises
> Name of vineyard
> Quality control number

The EEC Commission permits mention of only seven of the many varieties of Portuguese grapes on the approved form of label. These are: Alvarinho, Avesso, Azal branco, Espadeira, Arinto and Ramisco.

The Ministerial Order of 11 August 1979 also contains very detailed provisions as to the making of 'Quality Rosé Wines' (a description as yet permissible only in Portugal), listing hundreds of parishes in the provinces of Trás-os-Montes, Beira Alta, Beira

Baixa, Beira Litoral, Estremadura, Ribatejo, Alentejo and Algarve—from the far north to the southern extreme of the country—within whose boundaries the vines may be grown, and also some two dozen approved grape varieties. It would seem that these recommendations have yet to be recognized by the EEC Commission for Portuguese wine sold in the Community; and the schedule is in any case in abeyance in the case of the big firms, 'which, because of large-scale trade, cannot, without serious risks, fulfil within the time limit . . . the provisions established in the present Ministerial order'.

As regards fortified dessert wines, such as Port, Madeira and Moscatel de Setúbal, no set form of Community labelling has yet been laid down by the EEC Commission; and as Portugal and Spain are the two parties most interested, this is a matter which may well await their eventual entry into the Common Market. However, when sold in Britain, such wines must still comply with the UK's own rules and carry on their labels:

Name of the drink

Name and head office address of the bottler (or of a seller established within the Community)

Place/country of origin

Nominal volume

Alcoholic strength.

When inspecting a Portuguese wine list the first thing is to decide whether you wish to drink one of the *pétillant* 'green wines' or *vinhos verdes* or a *vinho maduro* (a 'mature wine'), such as Dão; the two types are often listed separately. Some of the terms commonly appearing on wine labels are:

Tinto	Full-bodied red
Clarete	Light red
Rosado	Rosé (often lightly carbonated)
Branco	White
Espumante	Sparkling
Generoso	An apéritif or dessert wine high in alcohol
Licoroso	Fortified
Vinho de mesa	Table wine
Doce } *Suave* }	Sweet

36

Seco	Dry
Meio Seco	Medium-dry
Bruto	Extra-dry (used only of sparkling wines)
Velho	Old
Reserva	Mature wine of good quality
Garrafeira	A select wine with long bottle age, e.g. Garrafeira 1970
Colheita/Colh.	Vintage, e.g. Colh. 1975
Aguardente/ Aguardente de Vinho	Brandy
Bagaceira/ Aguardente de Bagaceira	A potent spirit distilled, like *marc*, from grapeskins and pips
Região Demarcada	Demarcated region
Adega	As with the Spanish *bodega*, a concern which has made and/or shipped and sold the wine
Cava, Caves	*Literally* a cellar, but used of establishments making sparkling wines

2

Port

Porto ('port') or, in its anglicized form, Oporto has rightly given its name to the wine for which it is famous all over the world. Port starts its life in the terraced vineyards of the high Douro valley; the young wine was formerly ferried down the fast-flowing river; and after it has come of age in the Lodges of Vila Nova de Gaia, facing the city proper across the wide ravine of the Douro, it must be shipped over the curving sand bar at the mouth if it is to be entitled to the name.

The city is the second in Portugal and its long history began when the Romans founded Portus Cale on the site of an even earlier settlement. It now bears much the same relationship to Lisbon as does Barcelona to Madrid. In the words of an old saw, 'Lisbon plays, Coimbra studies, Braga prays, Oporto works.' Among its most famous sons was Prince Henry the Navigator who sailed against the Moors at Ceuta in 1415, true to Oporto's continuing reputation as a cradle of liberty, later so vividly demonstrated by popular opposition to the French invaders during the Peninsular War.

It is also perhaps in character that Oporto's most notable monuments are commercial: the ornate nineteenth-century Palacio de Bolsa with its extraordinary Arabian Hall, encrusted with Moorish-style tiles; Eiffel's frail railway bridge; and the cavernous, red-roofed Port Lodges lining the south bank of the river. Not least impressive is the foursquare granite Factory House in the former Rua dos Inglezes ('Street of the English'), built during the last years of the eighteenth century as a meeting place for the British merchants or Factors and now used as a club for the senior partners of the thirteen British Port shippers. Apart from its fine reception rooms and furniture, the building contains relics like a visitors' book with the names of Wellington's officers who were made honorary members during the Peninsular War and a complete file of *The Times* dating from its opening. It also houses twin dining rooms, each laid for the same meal, to the second of which the members and their guests adjourn for dessert so that they may enjoy their Port away from the aromas of cooking.

The Factory House is a symbol of the 'Britishness' which has pervaded the trade in port since the English merchants migrated from Viana do Castelo during the seventeenth century to open up the trade in wines from the Douro valley. The oldest of the Port firms is said to be that of C. N. Kopke & Co. Ltd, founded in 1638 by Christian Kopke, the first consul-general for the Hanseatic Free Towns. The senior English concern is Warre & Co., founded under a different name about 1670; and Croft & Co., which first traded under the name of Phayre & Bradley, is almost as old. During the next century and a half English and Scots names followed thick and fast: Quarles Harris (1680); Taylor, Fladgate and Yeatman (originally founded by the Bearsley family in 1692); Morgan Bros. (1713); Offley Forrester (c. 1729); Hunt Roope (1735); Sandeman (1790); Graham (1814); and Cockburns (1815).

Some account of the evolution of Port from a rough beverage wine has already been given (p. 23), but it was a slow process conducted largely by trial and error until Louis Pasteur was able to provide a rational explanation for the processes of fermentation in the mid-nineteenth century. George Robertson, in his scholarly *Port*, credits the first successful attempts to produce a smooth and palatable wine by brandying it during fermentation to the abbot of a monastery in Lamego around 1678, but for many years after this it was more common to add brandy *after* fermentation or to add it in insufficient amount, when fermentation would later begin anew. Again, the importance of ageing was not properly understood, and there are few drinks as fiery as a doctored wine with which the brandy has not been completely blended—as witness the 'red biddy', later served as a Port substitute in Victorian pubs. When matters were compounded by the addition of the ill-famed elderberry juice, it is not surprising that claret-drinkers in England should have greeted it with jingles such as:

39

George Sandeman, founder of the famous Port firm.
(Geo. G. Sandeman & Co. Ltd.)

Mark how it smells. Methinks, a real pain
Is by its colour thrown upon my brain.
I've tasted it—'tis spiritless and flat
And has as many different tastes
As can be found in compound pastes . . .
But fetch us a pint of any sort,
Navarre, Galicia, anything but Port.

In 1727 the English merchants in Oporto decided to coordinate
their efforts to improve the wine and founded the Association of

40

Port Wine Shippers. Nevertheless, in 1754 its agents in the vineyards were writing:

The English merchants knew that the first-rate wine of the Factory had become excellent; but they wished to exceed the limits Nature had assigned to it, and that, when drunk, it should feel like liquid fire in the stomach; that it should burn like inflamed gunpowder; that it should have the tint of ink; that it should be like the sugar of Brazil in sweetness, and like the spices of India in aromatic flavour. They began by recommending, by way of secret, that it was proper to dash it with Brandy in the fermentation to give it strength; and with elderberries, or the rind of the ripe grape, to give it colour . . .

In the circumstances, and in the face of high-handed demands on the growers by the Association, the Marquês de Pombal's dramatic intervention in 1756 seems to have been well justified; and during its earlier years his Oporto Wine Company carried out many beneficial reforms. The use of elderberry juice was outlawed; a monopoly of the spirit used for fortifying the wine resulted in a better quality of brandy; the farmers received fair payment for their grapes and exports were sensibly regulated. In 1780 the Company cleared the massive slabs of granite from the rapids of the Cachão de Valeira above Pinhão, so making navigation of the river safer for the *barcos rabelos* used for ferrying the new wine from the *quintas* in the Upper Douro to the Lodges in Vila Nova de Gaia. And, above all, the strict demarcation of the region and its division into two areas, one supplying wine for export and the other for home consumption, was a major step forward.

As time went by, corruption in the state monopoly became rife, even the Marquês de Pombal shipping wine to Oporto from his estate in Carcavelos near Lisbon and passing it off as Port; and it fell to a young Englishman, J. J. Forrester, who had arrived in Porto in 1831, to join his uncle's firm of Offley Forrester & Co., to play a major role in perfecting the wine as we know it today. In 1844 the lively and contentious Forrester set the shippers by the ears with the publication of his pamphlet, *A Word or Two on Port Wine*, in which he roundly accused the trade of adulterating the wines with sugar, *geropiga* (or sweet must) and the ever-recurrent elderberry juice. He was also a rooted opponent of brandying the

The Baron Forrester, who pioneered improvements in making Port during the early nineteenth century. (Contemporary painting)

wine. In this he was fortunately overruled, but his contributions—not least the detailed mapping of the Douro River from the Spanish frontier to its mouth—were so outstanding that he was eventually created a Baron by a grateful Portuguese government.

Climate, soil and grapes

The demarcated region extends for some 100 kilometres, following the course of the Douro River from the Spanish frontier to a point rather below Régua and Lamego and across the valleys of its tributaries—the Corgo, Torto, Pinhão and the others—with a maximum breadth of about 45 kilometres.

At first sight the wild and picturesque Upper Douro valley, with its deep gorge flanked by steep and rocky mountains, its blistering summers and biting winter rains, would appear unsuited for any form of agriculture. It is possible to plant vineyards only because the vine is exceptionally well-adapted to grow in poor soils, its roots reaching deep for any available moisture, and also because of the astonishing human effort which has gone into constructing fertile terraces on the precipitous slopes. In more ways than one it may be said that Port is an artefact.

The best ways to survey the region are either by way of the train from Régua to Barca de Alva on the Spanish frontier, which threads its way up the valley along a narrow ledge blasted out of the rock at water-level, crossing and recrossing the river, or by boat. Not long ago I made the trip by water, in one of the old high-prowed vessels, from the Quinta de Meão, some 40 kilometres short of the Spanish border, to the great new lock at Valeira, east of Pinhão.

This is one of the most rugged and precipitous stretches of the river, with great creviced cliffs, carpeted with shrubs and wild flowers wherever they can find a foothold and dropping sheer to the dark flow of the river. Only occasionally, as around Ferreira's

The high valley of the Douro near Meão and the Spanish border.
(Jan Read)

Quinta do Vesúvio, the largest of the great mansions built by the Port families, does the land fall back to allow for terraces of vines and olives. Just short of the lock we left the sunshine and entered the gloomy gorge of the Cachão de Valeira, now a smooth but sinister stretch of black water. It was here that the Baron Forrester met his death in 1862 in suitably dramatic fashion when he was returning from a lunch with the Baroness Fladgate and the redoubtable Dona Antónia Adelaide Ferreira, uncrowned queen of the Douro and its largest property owner. Their boat capsized in the rapids, and the ladies, buoyed up by their crinolines, were swept ashore, but Forrester, weighed down by a belt containing gold sovereigns for the payment of his farmers, sank without a trace.

Lower down the river, around Pinhão, the valley opens out, and the white *quintas*—Croft's Quinta da Roeda, the Quinta do Noval,

Dona Antónia Adelaide Ferreira, uncrowned Queen of the Douro and the largest landowner in the region during the nineteenth century. (Contemporary painting)

Terraced Port vineyards near Pinhão. (Jan Read)

Warre's Quinta do Bonfim and the others—lie among their neatly terraced vineyards. The demarcated area, covering some 240,000 hectares, is divided into three sub-regions, from west to east, Baixo Corgo, Cima Corgo and Douro Superior; and it is in fact the Cima Corgo around Pinhão which produces the choicest wines.

Both the soil and climate vary progressively across the region. In general, the soil is volcanic and is characterized by the presence of a flaky pre-Cambrian schist rich in phosphate, and also containing plenty of potassium, but very little nitrate, organic material or lime. Progressing eastwards towards the Spanish border, the content of schist increases, and though the fertility of these schistous soils is low, it is from them that the best wines are made. The construction of the traditional terraces involves both the building of a retaining wall and the further preparation of the soil to receive the vines, both by blasting and elbow grease. That the terraces exist at all is owing to the past availability of cheap and plentiful labour; under present conditions, even their maintenance poses problems, and near Régua whole hillsides were abandoned after the phylloxera epidemic of the 1870s and are now left uncultivated or given over to olives. In recent years there have

45

been experiments with sloping, unterraced vineyards, like those of the Rhine valley. These are so steep that they cannot be worked with tractors and must be tilled by means of a winch, but are proving their worth.

Most of the rain falls between November and March, penetrating the schistous rock and forming a reservoir when it reaches an impermeable layer below. During the blistering summers, when temperatures may reach as much as 45°C, there is little or no rain, so that it is the stored moisture which keeps the vines alive and healthy. The Upper Douro is sheltered from the rain-bearing clouds of the Atlantic by the mountain barrier of the Serra do Marão, and across the region itself rainfall decreases from east to west, while summer temperatures increase, as is apparent from the table.

Towns (west to east)	Average annual temperature (°C)	Average annual rainfall (mm)
Oporto	16	1200
Régua	18	900
Pinhão	19	700
Moncorvo	20	500
Barca de Alva	21	400

Of the three sub-regions, the area planted with vines comprises 28·8 per cent of the Baixa Corgo, 9·7 per cent of the Cima Corgo and only 3·0 per cent of the Douro Superior. The figures in the table and the high amount of schist in the soil explain the low productivity in the mountainous eastern area—though the quality of the grapes is high.

More than forty different varieties of grape—twenty-eight of them red and nineteen white—are used for making Port, whereas in Jerez there are only three main varieties of vine. The reason appears to be that the climate and soils are much more uniform in Jerez, and in the winding valleys of the Douro and its tributaries the different micro-climates and soils favour some varieties more than others. Again, in a properly balanced Port, the colour of, say, the Sousão, the sweetness and aroma of the Rufete, the richness of the Tinta Francisca and the good yield of the Touriga all play their part.

The official classification lists the following grapes in the first category (the others are classified as 'good' or 'average'):

Red	White
Red	*White*
Bastardo	Donzelinho
Donzelinho Tinto	Esgana-Cão
Mourisco	Folgosão
Touriga Francesa	Gouveio or Verdelho
Tinta Roriz	Malvasia Fina
Tinta Francisca	Malvasia Rei
Tinto Cão	Rabigato
Touriga Nacional	Viosinho

It seems likely that most of the vines now used in the Douro were of French origin. The history of one, at least, the popular Tinta Francisca, is well-established and dates back to the seventeenth century, when the proprietor of the Quinta de Roriz, a Scot by the name of Robert Archibald, sent his son to Burgundy to bring back cuttings of the red Pinot Noir. Roriz still produces perhaps the best musts of the whole Douro from dark black grapes with hard skins and high sugar content. Although the present proprietor of the Quinta de Roriz, Pedro van-Zeller, does not himself make wine commercially, the superb quality of the fruit may be tasted in wines such as the beautiful twenty-year-old 'Duque de Bragança' tawny from Ferreira.

Apart from the large vineyards owned by the big shippers, there are some 85,000 smallholdings in the Douro farmed by about 25,000 growers. The body responsible for their supervision and for maintaining the standards of viticulture is the Casa do Douro, with its headquarters in Régua. One of its most important tasks is to decide, in the interests of quality and in the light of demand, how much Port may be made in any particular year. This is done on the basis of a classification of the vineyards and a points system, shown on page 48, assessing their capability for making good-quality wine.

According to the number of points awarded, the vineyards are classified in categories from A to F.

The Instituto do Vinho do Porto authorizes the shippers to export not more than one-third of their stocks annually and obtains from them an accurate estimate of the new wine required to make good this amount. In consultation with the Casa do Douro, it then fixes the total amount of Port to be made in a particular year, and individual growers are allotted a quota according to their category in the official classification. In practice, growers in Categories A and B will make as much wine as they are able, and the others progressively less according to their place in the table. Only about 40 per cent of the wine from the region is made into Port, of which the production in an average year is some 80,000 pipes or 445,000 hectolitres.

POINT SYSTEM ASSESSING VINEYARDS

		Maximum points
(a)	Production	120
(b)	Soil	180
(c)	Gradient	100
(d)	Altitude	150
(e)	Geographical position	600
(f)	Climatic environment	210
(g)	Upkeep and maintenance	100
(h)	Qualities of grapes	150
(i)	Age of vines	70
		1680

Vinification and elaboration

Harvesting begins in mid-September in the Cima Corgo and two or three weeks later in parts of the Baixa Corgo; and the wine was traditionally fermented in massive open tanks or *lagares* made of solid granite, with a capacity of up to twenty or thirty pipes. It was—and still is, where it survives—a picturesque ceremony, with gangs of men (the official number was two per pipe) treading the grapes with their bare feet and later submerging the *manta* (or cap) with wooden paddles called *macacos*. Rupert Croft-Cooke has vividly described in *Port* this climax of the wine-maker's year:

> Now the band strikes up, now every man moves in the purple must, which covers his knees. Grinning, shouting, dancing alone or in couples face to face, twining their arms above their heads in curious serpentine movements, they never cease treading. . . . They are satyrs, they are crazy Bacchants, they have ceased to be quite human . . .

48

You will still see the great *lagares* in all the *quintas* belonging to the large shippers, some of whom, like Ferreira, still make limited use of them, since they consider that the wine made in them is of special quality. Among the most impressive are those in the firm's *quinta* at Meão (see also p. 125), far up the valley and constructed by the famous Dona Antónia Adelaide Ferreira in 1892 as one of her most grandiose projects.

In the larger *quintas* the great bulk of the wine is nowadays fermented in cement vats or, as at Sandemans, in stainless steel tanks. The most commonly used type is employed in combination with a mechanical crusher and constructed on the principle of a coffee percolator so as to ensure continuous automatic submersion of the skins and pips. First used in Algeria, the vats are made of concrete coated with epoxy resin and contain a sleeved tube or *autovinificador* and a pipe through which the fermenting must is at intervals forced up by the pressure of carbon dioxide gas into an open reservoir at the top. When sufficient must has been forced out, a valve opens to release the gas, whereupon the must flows back into the vat and is sprinkled over the floating cap through the *autovinificador*.

Whatever the method of fermentation, it is cut short once the appropriate amount of sugar has been converted to alcohol and the specific gravity reaches 1·045 and the Degree Baumé 6·2° by running off the wine into fresh containers and adding grape spirit. The *aguardente* used for this purpose is not brandy such as that made by many of the Port firms, but a spirit of 77° strength made by the government-controlled Administración Geral de Alcool (AGE) by distilling wine from various parts of the country in a continuous column (like those used in making grain whisky). It is usually added in the proportion of 110 litres of *aguardente* to 440 litres of must.

The new wine is then left to rest at the *quinta* for some months while the spirit amalgamates with it. For many years it was run off into pipes to be ferried down the rapids of the Douro to the Port Lodges of Vila Nova de Gaia in the sharp-prowed *barcos rabelos*, with their single, high square sail—a few survivors are moored opposite the Lodges. The practice began to die out with the construction of a railway line to Régua and Pinhão in the centre of the region, and now in turn the trains headed by the old, tall-chimneyed steam locomotives, affectionately christened the

Paciencia, have yielded to tanker lorries, making laborious progress along the winding uphill and downhill road to Oporto.

The lodges at least retain much of their traditional atmosphere. Rambling, old-fashioned buildings with red-tiled roofs supported by shrunken beams, they stand cheek by jowl along the granite quays of the Douro and climb the hill behind. Most incorporate a cavernous cooper's shop, where the pipes are fabricated and repaired on the premises—though the art is in somewhat of a decline now that so much Port is bottled in the Lodge or shipped in metal containers. At Ferreira there is a period shop, engulfed in the middle of the Lodge when it was extended years ago by roofing over one of the narrow streets (it is now used as a lounge for visitors); but the heart of any Lodge is the modern tasting room and laboratory, to which samples of each and every wine from the *quinta* are submitted on arrival and where its final style and method of elaboration are decided, and its subsequent development is regularly checked and recorded.

In the seemingly endless and interconnected cellars, you will find a bewildering array of receptacles for ageing and maturing the wine. These include cement vats where the *lotes*, or parcels of new

Balseiros *in the lodge of Delaforce Sons and Cª. in Vila Nova de Gaia.* (*Jan Read*)

wine from the *quinta*, are first allowed to rest and modern stainless steel tanks used for blending. Of the more traditional wooden containers, made from oak, Brazilian mahogany or chestnut, there are *balseiros*, large vats on legs like the Spanish *tinos*; *toneis*, very large barrels; and pipes in various sizes—630 litres, 550 litres and 534 litres for shipping; and also the smaller hogsheads and quarter-casks. As to which are used in maturing the wines, the guiding principle is that the smaller the cask, the more rapid oxidation and maturation. Only Portuguese oak is employed for the long-term maturation of fine Ports.

Styles of Port

The aristocrat of the wines is, of course, **vintage Port**, made exclusively of wines from the best vineyards, all of one particularly good year. *Lotes* of different wines are first aged in lodge lot casks of 630 litres or in oak *balseiros* for two years, after which they are blended and bottled. It was once the custom to ship the wine to London for bottling, but the practice has been in decline over the last decade (see Appendix 3), and since 1975 all vintage Port has been bottled at the Lodges.

The declaration of a vintage year is a matter of great moment, taken only after careful examination of samples of the wine submitted to the Instituto do Vinho do Porto. Different firms often concur in declaring a vintage, since climatic conditions over the wine-growing area as a whole are generally much the same; but micro-climate naturally affects the issue.

In 1868, only Crofts failed to declare, a decision taken after an examination of the parched vineyards. Its director, J. R. Wright, left for Oporto on mule-back shortly before a fine rain set in and subsequently refused to change his decision. He nevertheless reaped a late benefit by selling the wine as '1869 Vintage' in a year when his rivals were unable to offer a vintage Port. There have, on the other hand, been occasions on which only one or two of the firms have declared, such as 1931, the year of an outstanding Quinta Noval, when only two shippers declared; and a 'general' declaration by all of the companies is relatively rare. Of the more recent years some of the best were 1945, 1947, 1948, 1955, 1958, 1960, 1963, 1966, 1970, 1975 and 1977. For more detailed information with an assessment of the character of the wines, the reader is referred to George Robertson's *Port* and to Sarah Bradford's *The Englishman's Wine.*

Vintage Port throws a crust or sediment in bottle and must be decanted. Contrary to popular belief, it will not keep indefinitely and it is unwise to buy vintage Port that is more than thirty years old without sampling it. However, a great deal depends upon the shipper, the wines from Taylor, for example, ageing exceptionally well and slowly.

Late bottled vintage Port is so called because it is kept longer in wood—usually for about five years—than the straight vintage Port, which it resembles in consisting entirely of wine of the same year, though it is, of course, a blend from different vineyards. The label should state the year of bottling as well as the vintage.

Vintage character Port, despite the name, is not blended from wines of the same vintage, but from first-class Cima Corgo wines, not all of which were necessarily made in vintage years. It much resembles another top-quality wine, **Crusted Port**, no longer made in Oporto itself. Like vintage Port, this throws a crust or deposit, as the name implies, but it differs from it in being a blend of *lotes* of different age and in being bottled after rather longer in the wood, hence maturing more quickly. It has perhaps not quite the same balance and tends to be shorter-lived; but it requires a connoisseur to tell the difference.

Tawny Port differs radically from the above types, since it is a blend of different vintages which have undergone prolonged maturation in cask. The resulting slow aeration through the pores of the wood results in a paler, less fully bodied and more aromatic wine, preferred by people who find the vintage and vintage character Ports too rich and heavy. Fine old tawnies, such as Delaforce's ten-year-old 'His Eminence's Choice' or Ferreira's twenty-year-old 'Duque de Bragança', are in the nature of things expensive, and younger, much inferior tawnies, without the same nose and flavour, are sometimes made by blending red and white Ports. Once bottled, tawny Ports do not improve with age.

Because of the relative infrequency of declarations, the great bulk of Port shipped abroad is **wood Port**, defined as a blended wine matured in cask until it is ready for drinking. The aristocrat of wood Ports is tawny, but most of such wine emerges as **ruby**. The younger rubies are aged for only two or three years and are the basic Port lovers' wines, being relatively inexpensive and possessing an attractive and full-bodied freshness. Others are given much longer in wood and are made from dark wines, so that they are in effect something like the vintage character wines. Inexpensive ruby was once a favourite tipple in English pubs, especially when mixed with lemonade in the 'ladylike' form of 'port and lemon'.

All of these Ports are made basically from black grapes; but there are also **white Ports**, also matured in wood. For these the method of fermentation differs in that the skins are separated from the must at an early stage, as the wine would otherwise pick up too much colour; they are not, however, any less strong in alcohol. The traditional white Ports are sweet or very sweet, and generally less satisfying than the reds as an after dinner drink. However, the shippers have more recently introduced dry white Ports made by fermenting out the grapes before brandying the wine, and, without making much inroad on the foreign market for sherry, have gone to considerable lengths to popularize it as an alternative. When it actually *is* dry, as in the case of wines which I have tasted from Taylor's, Cockburn's and Croft's, it is a somewhat metallic, but not unacceptable apéritif—though (to my mind) it lacks the crispness of a *fino* sherry or the character of a good Sercial Madeira. Despite the label, some of the wines possess a residual sweetness and are much improved when chilled and drunk with a twist of lemon.

Exports and shippers

The boom in the Port trade following the First World War has never been matched since, and Port has undergone vagaries in popularity in recent decades. It has never been widely drunk in Portugal itself; but habits are changing and there is a steady upswing in sales at home and on the continent to compensate for a reduced market in England. France, where the taste is for drinking sweet wines before meals, takes more than any other country in terms of bulk; but England remains by far the most important customer for vintage Port, which, though accounting for only some 2 per cent of total production, remains the most profitable form of export. At the time of writing, demand for vintage Port outstrips demand.

In all, the Port Wine Shippers Association numbers 42 members. Some of the famous old firms have been taken over by the big wine and brewery combines or have amalgamated, but most have maintained the name and individuality of the wines. The following is a list of some of the better-known names:

Bermester	Martinez Gassiot
Butler Nephew	Morgan
Cálem	Niepoort
Cockburn Smithes	Offley Forrester
Croft	Quarles Harris
Delaforce	Quinta do Noval
Diez Hermanos	Rebello Valente (the vintage
Dow	mark for Robertson Brothers)
Ferreira	Robertson Bros.
Feuerheed	Sandeman
Fonseca	Smith Woodhouse
Gonzalez Byass	Taylor, Fladgate & Yeatman
Gould Campbell	Tuke, Holdsworth
Graham	Hunt, Roope
Kopke	van Zeller
Mackenzie	Warre

In addition to these household names, many well-known British wine merchants ship vintage Port and bottle it under their names; while Harvey's (which owns Cockburn's) sell wood Ports under its own label.

3

Madeira

Jack! how agrees the devil and thee about thy soul, that thou
soldest him on Good Friday last for a cup of Madeira and a
cold capon's leg?

SHAKESPEARE, *King Henry IV*, Part I

It seems that Shakespeare was guilty of anachronism in suggest-
ing that Sir John Falstaff drank either sack or Madeira, since at
the time of his bibulous excesses the Madeira archipelago was as
yet unexplored and lay shrouded in what an early Portuguese
seafarer described as 'vapour rising out of the mouth of hell'.

The island was discovered in 1419 by João Gonçalves Zarco and
Tristão Vaz Teixera, the leaders of an expedition despatched by
Prince Henry the Navigator, who named it *a ilha da madeira*
because of the dense woods which covered its precipitous and
uninhabited mountains. The early Portuguese colonists set fire to
the trees to clear the soil and set about the construction of the
poios (or terraces) so typical of Madeira today. The first crop was
sugar cane, introduced from Sicily; and somewhat later the
Cretan Malvasia (or Malmsey) vine was imported from Portugal.
It is on record that wine was being exported to Europe by 1460,
and a century later it was a favourite at the court of François I and
is said to have been drunk by Bluff King Hal at the Field of the
Cloth of Gold; but the history of Madeira as we know it begins
when the Portuguese government harboured Prince Rupert's fleet
after the defeat of Charles I by the forces of the Commonwealth.
This caused war between the two countries, and one of the
conditions of the peace treaty signed in 1654 was that English
merchants should be granted special privileges. By 1708 they were
so numerous as to establish a 'Factory'; and, like Port, Madeira,
as we now know it, was evolved as the result of political
contingency and was perfected by the English settlers.

At the time England was preoccupied with the conquest and exploitation of her colonies in the West Indies and North America. To safeguard her commercial interests, it was decreed by an ordinance of Charles II in 1663 that nothing produced in Europe might be shipped to the plantations or colonies except in English vessels and from English ports. The colonists were at one with the English wine merchants and discovered a loophole in the regulations: Madeira, after all, was an island off the coast of Africa. During the eighteenth and nineteenth centuries dozens of British wine firms established themselves on the island; the sugar canes were rooted up and replaced by vines; and ever-increasing amounts of wine were shipped, especially to the eastern seaboard of the United States. It is for this reason that Madeira is still best appreciated and understood in America.

In his book *Madeira*—which remains essential reading for those interested in the history of the wine—Rupert Croft-Cooke has an amusing story illustrating the close rapport between the colonists and the shippers:

> All over British America it had been a recognized practice for the Customs Officers to permit merchants and shipmasters to enter only a part of their imported cargoes in the books of the Customs Houses, and to land the remainder without payment.
>
> The Commissioners resolved to put a stop to this, and when the sloop *Liberty*, belonging to Hancock, arrived at Boston laden with Madeira wine, the Captain as usual proposed to the tide-waiter who came on board to inspect it, that part should be put ashore duty free. This suggestion was refused.
>
> The tide-waiter then became 'violent' so Hancock locked him in a cabin and proceeded to land the whole cargo. When the Commissioners heard what was happening they caused the sloop to be arrested, on which the crowd ashore became violent and assaulted the Customs Officers detailed to make the arrest. Next day they smashed the Inspector General's windows, dragged his boat through the town and made a public bonfire of it. The Commissioners and Customs Officers had to take refuge in Castle William.

Of the British merchants who gave their names to the famous shippers of today, two of the first to arrive were John Leacock, in 1741, the orphan son of a London weaver, and then a young Scot,

Francis Newton, whose firm of Newton, Gordon, Murdoch and Scott now trades as Cossart Gordon & Co.

By the end of the eighteenth century, Madeira was more popular in England than Port. Quoting from the Apsley Papers, Philip Guedalla wrote that 'military manners prescribed officially a monthly ration of fifteen bottles of Madeira as the bare limit of necessity', and the wine was later the favourite of the Prince Regent. During the period of the Napoleonic Wars, the island was occupied by British troops. Among them was their quartermaster, John Blandy, who remained to found one of the most famous of Madeira firms. Other arrivals at about the same time were William Cossart, an Irishman of Huguenot stock, who joined forces with Francis Newton, and a Scot, William Grant, founder of the great firm now trading as Rutherford, Miles & Co.

To begin with, the wines were unfortified; but because of hostility during the reign of Queen Anne, few British vessels put in at the islands, and the storage problem became so acute that the merchants perforce began to distil the surplus wine into brandy. Somewhat later this was added to the wine, so enabling it to withstand the long sea passage across the Atlantic. In 1753 Francis Newton, complaining of the methods employed by his competitors, writes: 'I really impute the complaints I have of wines to my not putting a Bucket or two of Brandy in each pipe as other houses do.' However, it was not long before all the successful exporters were fortifying their wine. It was further found that when casks were transported in a small sailing ship, the shaking and the heat of the equator softened the wine by helping the spirit to amalgamate with it.

Whatever the final destination, it then became the practice to despatch it on a long sea voyage. Thus, Cyrus Redding, writing in 1851, quotes the freight per pipe to England as 20s. to 25s. direct, £7 by way of the East Indies, £4 4s. by the West Indies, and £5 to £6 via the Brazils. The effects of the voyage were later achieved artificially by stoving, and Redding describes how 'A pipe of Madeira has been attached to the beam of a steam-engine, in the engine house, where the temperature is always high and the motion continual, and in a year it could not be known from the choicest East India.'

Soil, grapes and elaboration

The island is volcanic in origin and the best soil is light red in colour, consisting of a mixture of the light *saibro* and *pedro molle* with clay and volcanic cinder. Prior to the double calamities of oidium and phylloxera, from which the trade has never fully recovered, a large variety of grapes was grown, including the once prolific Negra Mole, the Moscatel and also the Terrantez, which makes a very individual, though somewhat steely wine. Although a number of American hybrids, introduced after the phylloxera epidemic and now frowned upon by the EEC Commission, are still used for making 'cooking Madeira' and a poor red beverage wine, for the purposes of the better Madeiras four main grapes survive today, and their names are used to describe the wines: in increasing order of sweetness, Sercial, Verdelho (said to be the same as the Pedro Ximénez of Jerez), Bual and Malmsey.

The vines are grown in small terraced plots known as *poios* and in trellises some 2 metres high, thus permitting the cultivation of vegetables underneath. Water has always been short and is channelled down from the mountains in narrow courses called *levadas*, from which it is strictly rationed. The best of the growths come from the south of the island, especially from the parishes of San Antonio Campanário, San Amaro, Ponto de Pargo, Estreito and Câma de Lobos. It was at this seaside village west of the capital, Funchal, that Sir Winston Churchill was in the habit of setting up his easel to paint. It is famous for the Negra Mole grape, used for making Tinta, the strong red wine so liked by the Victorians under the name of 'Tent'. Vines are also grown on the neighbouring island of Porto Santos, but the wine is unremarkable and used for blending.

Harvesting begins in mid-August with the Malmsey, Bual and Tinta grapes planted on the lower slopes; the Sercials on the higher and cooler slopes are not picked until October. The grapes were traditionally trodden barefoot in stone troughs and the must was brought down to Funchal in goat-skins, slung across the shoulders of the grower, draped across the back of a mule, or down the steep mountain tracks on oxen-drawn sledges—thus imparting to the wine the *borracho* taste so familiar to Richard Ford on the Spanish mainland.

Nowadays the grapes are transported to the *adegas* of the large

58

firms in trucks and crushed mechanically. The dry Madeiras—Sercial and Verdelho—are fermented out and fortified later; the sweet varieties—Bual and Malmsey—are made in much the same way as Port, by checking fermentation with spirit so as to leave residual sugar. The 'baking' of the *vinho claro* (new wine) in *estufas* continues virtually unchanged along the lines generally adopted in 1802. Government regulations lay down that it must be heated to 50°C for at least three months, or alternatively, to achieve more smoothness, to 45°C for a period of four months. The temperature may be increased by not more than 5°C each day. The less expensive wines are 'stoved' in tartrate-coated concrete tanks, holding up to 40,000 litres. Better-quality wines are 'stoved' in casks of American, Polish or Austrian oak in a heated concrete chamber, while the casks of the very best, destined for *reservas* and *soleras* are placed in the roof-space above the *estufa* to heat more gently. Alcohol, in the form of spirit rectified to 99·6 per cent, is added either before or after stoving, and the better wines are then matured in cask for three years, but benefit from much longer ageing in wood.

Almost all Madeiras are blends, and the best are matured in *solera* in the manner of sherry, sometimes remaining in oak for as long as twenty-five years, and usually undergo further blending before bottling and shipment. Since a certain amount of alcohol is lost in the *estufa*, the cheapest of the sweet wines are fermented out and then fortified and sweetened with an *arrobe* made by boiling down must. To make good any loss of alcohol, current Madeiras are fortified to 17 per cent and brought up to 18 per cent before shipment.

Of all wines, Madeira most improves with really prolonged maturation in bottle. This is not a fetish, as with the hundred-year-old clarets sold for ridiculous prices in the auction room and as often as not faded or turbid and undrinkable. Of course the wine must be sound and carefully made in the first place; when it is, it becomes steadily more concentrated in flavour, ending up (like Tokay) more as an essence than a wine for ordinary drinking. Raymond Postgate describes how he drank a 1795 Terrantez 'in full and even excessive vigour'; and at a banquet at Reid's Hotel in Funchal, Winston Churchill once held up his glass of Bual and remarked: 'Do you realize that this wine was made when Marie Antoinette was still alive?' One of the best-made Madeiras which I have myself drunk, at the invitation of Ronald Avery in Bristol, was a pre-phylloxera Sercial, bone-dry, fragrant and crisp.

It was formerly the custom, as it still is with Port, to make vintage Madeiras from grapes harvested in the same year. These splendid wines are still made in very limited amount; in their heyday the wines sent to the United States were often and picturesquely named after the vessel and year in which they were shipped. Thus Rupert Croft-Cooke cites 'The *All Saints* 1791' and the '*Rapid* 1817'.

Types of Madeira

When choosing a Madeira, the first thing to look for is the name of the grape, which determines the style of the wine. There has, however, been considerable abuse of varietal names, and many of the wines have been made only partially from grapes of the variety that appears on the label. Regulations are being tightened, but the reputation of the shipper remains all-important. Madeiras, like white Ports, are rarely as dry as a *fino* sherry, nor should one expect them to be. Because of evaporation and ullage and the time involved in making them, good Madeiras are anything but inexpensive, but in my own experience the maturer wines repay the money spent on them.

The driest of Madeiras, **Sercial**, is thought to have originated from a Riesling grape, but bears little similarity to other wines made from it. The must is fermented slowly and to completion so as to consume most of the sugar, and the spirit is added gradually and in instalments. It should be aged for at least eight years and is best drunk as an apéritif or with soup.

Verdelho is sweeter than Sercial, but may still be drunk at the beginning of a meal. With a slice of Madeira cake, an English confection devised to set off the wines, it is a most welcome alternative to 11 o'clock coffee or afternoon tea.

Bual and **Malmsey**, made by adding sufficient spirit to arrest fermentation and to leave a considerable amount of sugar in the wine, are sweeter and heavier. They are usually drunk as dessert wines, and Malmsey is the fruitier and more unctuous of the two. The Portuguese nevertheless drink Bual with the cheese; and in England there seems no reason why it should not be offered with Stilton as an alternative to Port.

There are other wines besides these four best-known, among them the picturesquely named 'Rainwater'. According to one legend, a consignment of casks awaiting shipment to America was inundated with rain and the contents diluted. The wine was despatched in spite of this and met with such unexpected favour in Boston that the shippers set about reproducing it. A less romantic, but probably more accurate explanation is that given by Julian Jeffs in his *Wines of Europe*: namely that the grapes are 'grown high on the hillsides where there is no irrigation and the vines have to rely on the rainfall for their water'. It is, in fact, a light and fresh wine made from a blend of grapes varying from shipper to shipper.

In Victorian times the cheaper wines were marketed in London under a variety of names such as 'India Market', 'London Market', 'New York Market', 'Cargo' or 'Muslin Madeira'. One such survival was the 'London Particular', until recently sold by Avery of Bristol.

In May 1959, the famous house of Cossart Gordon & Co. Ltd held a tasting of nineteen wines, ranging from the Câma de Lobos 1789 and Terrantez 1795 to their 'youngest' vintage, a Verdelho 1810, noting that 'it might never be possible to assemble a similar collection of old Madeiras'. Nevertheless, their next tasting of the kind in 1979 was one that few of us who were privileged to attend will ever forget. The tasting notes are but a faint reflection of the beauty of the wines.

1. *Duo Centenary Celebration 1745–1945* (a blend of old *solera* Madeiras, each over sixty years). Light brick red, deep maderized nose, intensely fruity, long aftertaste.
2. *Bual Centenary Solera 1845* (The *solera* was laid down in the company's centenary year of 1845, and the wine was bottled from the wood in 1975.) Darker colour, very maderized nose, intense flavour, dryish finish.
3. *Bual Solera 1822* (The basis for this *solera* was the 1822 vintage, one of the best of the century.) Lighter colour, more restrained nose, surprising intensity, sweeter, beautiful.
4. *Malmsey Solera 1808* (probably the most highly regarded year ever for Malmsey, followed by 1822, 1880 and 1954). Brown colour, sweet, soft, very refined and round.
5. *Malmsey Vintage 1893* (The first vintage of note after the

phylloxera epidemic.) Brown, very pronounced maderized nose, intense very fruity flavour.

6. *Bual Vintage 1895* (From Câma de Lobos, the first good Bual vintage after the double scourges of oidium and phylloxera in 1852 and 1873.) Pale brown, light aromatic nose, silky, intense.

7. *Malmsey Vintage 1916* (Destined for Imperial Russia, but never shipped because of the Revolution of 1917.) Light elegant nose, dark colour, intense flavour.

8. *Malmsey Vintage 1920* (This Malmsey was considered to be as good as the famous 1880.) Drier, velvety and very stylish.

9. *Verdelho Vintage 1934* (Verdelho in this year was almost up to the standard of 1907.) Full, fresh, round on the palate, dry finish, most attractive.

10. *Sercial Vintage 1940* (From the best region for Sercial, 500 metres up above Estreito.) The nose and flavour were not as refined, still a lovely wine.

11. *Malmsey Vintage 1954* (Still relatively immature.) Sweet, and in comparison with the other wines, a bit flat and uncomplicated.

Exports and shippers

Total exports of Madeira in 1980 amounted to some 3,250,000 litres, of which 365,885 litres were bottled in the island. The largest markets for standard 'cooking Madeira', generally made from hybrid grapes, are France and West Germany. With imports of 116,634 litres, the United States is by far the biggest single importer of bottled Madeira, but Britain remains the best customer for the choice *solera* and vintage wines.

Many of the leading Madeira shippers have banded together as the Madeira Wine Association so as to maintain standards and share certain production facilities. At the time of writing, the member firms which ship to the United Kingdom are:

Blandy's Madeiras Lda.
Cossart Gordon & Co. Ltd
F. F. Ferraz Lda.
Freitas Martins Caldeira Lda.
Luís Gomes (Vinhos) Lda.

Leacock & Co. (Wine) Lda.
T. T. C. Lomelino Lda.
Rutherford and Miles
Shortridge Lawton & Co. Ltd

Other well-known firms are:

Adega Exportadores de Vinhos de Madeira
H. M. Borges
Henriques & Henriques
Marcelo Gomes & Cia. Lda.
Sandeman Sons & Co. Ltd
Veiga Franca & Co. Ltd
Vinhos Barbeito

Apart from the shippers in Madeira itself and their London agents, other good sources of Madeira in Britain are the old-established Bristol firms of Harveys and Averys.

4

Demarcated Wines of the Centre

There are four demarcated regions near Lisbon, all of them small and with a long tradition of wine-making, but nowadays of diminished importance because of their minuscule production. Except in the larger hotels and better restaurants, it is in fact difficult to find any of these wines, even in Portugal itself.

Carcavelos and Colares, on the Atlantic coast near the capital, face eventual extinction. When the vineyards were first planted, their proximity to a large market was a positive advantage; but the arduous business of making fine wine is now proving less profitable than the selling of plots to urban commuters for holiday villas.

Moscatel de Setúbal is made from grapes grown in the beautiful Arrábida Peninsula across the Tagus, an area threatened by the huge new shipyards and oil installations in the port of Setúbal and by industrial developments along the new motorway from Lisbon, although the present vogue for dry white wines seems to have resulted in no slackening of the demand for what remains one of the world's classical dessert wines.

There is no physical threat to the remaining district of Bucelas (the spelling 'Bucellas' on the labels is an antique version of the name), 24 kilometres north-west of Lisbon in the valley of the Trancão River; its delicate white wine is one of the best in Portugal, but the output is small.

BUCELAS

It seems on the cards that Shakespeare's Charneco came from Bucelas (see p. 22); apart from this, its white wines were

The vineyards of Caves Velhas near Bucelas. (Jan Read)

D. Fernando Porto Soares Franco of J. M. da Fonseca Sucrs. at a tasting of Moscatel de Setúbal, ranging from the current vintage to 1900 and earlier. (Jan Read)

popularized in England by officers of Wellington's army returning from the Peninsular War. Dickens referred to them in his *Sketches by Boz*, and they were the subject of Thomas Hood's uncomplimentary jingle:

> Bucelas made handy
> By Cape and bad brandy

Sugaring and brandying of the wine were, in fact, prevalent during the nineteenth century, but were forbidden when the region was demarcated in 1911 and control was vested in the União Vinícola Regional de Bucelas, a body now absorbed by the Junta Nacional do Vinho.

The vineyards, amounting only to some 182 hectares, centre on the Trancão River and are planted along the slopes and in the bottom of the valley in clay soils high in lime and sulphur. There are two grapes, the Arinto and Esgana Cão, and by law 65 per cent of the musts are made from the Arinto. Sometimes supposed to be a Riesling, introduced to the area either by the Marquês de Pombal or Teutonic crusaders, it produces wines quite unlike those of its native Germany.

Bucelas is nowadays made by only one concern, Camilo Alves, founded in 1881, which later acquired the firm of Caves Velhas; and it is under this label that it markets most of its wines, also including a range of good Dãos and some *garrafeiras* from the Ribatejo. Some 50 per cent of the grapes used for Bucelas are grown in the firm's own vineyards, the remainder being bought from independent farmers. After they are crushed, the must is allowed to settle in cement vats, and fermentation takes place in wooden *toneis* (or barrels) holding 3000 to 4000 litres. The wines are matured in *toneis* of Australian or Brazilian oak, up to 15,000 litres in capacity and some as old as eighty years, housed in the splendidly Victorian 'New Warehouse' in Bucelas, stone-built with great wooden roof trusses. The younger wines, of the type usually exported, are kept only a few months in wood, but the *garrafeiras* and those for the home market may spend up to years before being bottled.

The young Bucelas is a greenish straw-yellow in colour, with a delicate perfumed nose, light, dry and slightly acid, and contains between 11° and 12° of alcohol. It goes excellently with fish and other light dishes. With further age in wood and bottle, the wines become pronouncedly yellow and develop a banana flavour and very dry finish, at times lemony and at others reminiscent of bitter almonds. Average annual production is 6700 hectolitres.

CARCAVELOS

This is another wine which gained a reputation in England through a taste for it developed by Wellington's officers. It was already well-known in Portugal in the late eighteenth century, since the Marquês de Pombal—one of the country's most forceful statesmen, so powerful that, among his other reforms, he even confronted the Roman Catholic Church with the expulsion of the Jesuits—owned vineyards and a model winery at Oeras. It is less to his credit that, flouting his own regulations, he insisted on the blending of his wine with Port.

It is unfortunate that the dry summers and mild winters which so favoured the growth of the grapes should also have resulted in the explosive growth of Estoril, with near-by Cascais the most fashionable of Portugal's seaside resorts. Its linkage with Lisbon by 25 kilometres of urban motorway and the ensuing suburban development have resulted in the virtual disappearance of the vineyards; so what follows is mainly of historic interest.

The wines were made from a variety of grapes: the Galego Dourado, Boais, Arinto and Espadeiro, grown on soils in which limestone predominates, with small deposits of basalt. During the first half of the nineteenth century Carcavelos was producing 150,000 litres annually, but the onset of oidium devastated the vineyards and production in 1867 fell as low as 6370 litres. Another disaster followed in the shape of phylloxera. Thanks to the use of chemical sprays and American grafts, the position was eventually restored, and the region, or what remained of it, was demarcated in 1908 and administered by the União Vinícola Regional de Carcavelos, later absorbed by the Junta Nacional do Vinho.

Writing in 1929, P. Morton Shand described Carcavelos as 'a dryish-tasting fortified wine, topaz-coloured, with a peculiar almond flavour that is not usually appreciated at the first glass'. H. Warner Allen also commented on its 'curious nutty aroma'. Averaging 19° in strength, the wines vary from sweet to medium dry and are either drunk cold as a most individual apéritif or with a dessert.

The only remaining vineyards are those of the Quinta do Barão, belonging to Raul Ferreira & Filho, Lda., whose average annual production is 273 hectolitres.

COLARES

Colares differs from the other three demarcated regions near Lisbon in being first and foremost a producer of red wines; in fact it has traditionally made the best and most individual red wine of Portugal. It is now threatened, not only by the encroachment of commuters and week-enders from Lisbon, but by the high cost of labour resulting from the time-consuming and quite individual methods of viticulture.

Colares is a small town lying between the Atlantic coast and the heights of historic Sintra, dominated by the eccentric Neo-Manueline Pena Palace and the ruins of an old Moorish castle, and also the site of the beautiful medieval Royal Palace. Of its luxuriant, semi-tropical surroundings, Byron wrote in *Childe Harold*:

> The horrid crags by toppling convent crowned,
> The cork trees hoar that clothe the shaggy steep.
> The mountain moss by scorching skies imbrowned,
> The sunken glen, whose sunless shrubs must weep . . .

The history of Colares dates back to Roman times, and it was taken by the Moors in 1147. The earliest reference to its wine is in a decree made by the first king of Portugal, Afonso Henriques, in 1154. In 1255 King Afonso III made a grant of land to Pedro Miguel and his wife, Maria Estevão, stipulating that they must plant vines; and amongst his agricultural reforms, King Diniz in 1301 refers specifically to the making of wine in Colares. The tradition of wine-making continued through the centuries; but by the late nineteenth abuses had crept in and the wines were being adulterated by fortification with brandy in imitation of Port. From 1907 onwards a series of decrees was made, demarcating the region and outlawing such injurious practices; and in 1931 the Adega Regional de Colares was set up. By 1935 it numbered 507 *associados*, but its efforts to improve standards met with opposition from commercial interests, and there were firms which continued to buy cheap, badly made wine to the detriment of the growers as a whole. In what the official handbook of the region, *O Vinho de Colares*, describes as the 'Carta-Magna' of Colares Wine, a decree of 1934 finally empowered the Adega Regional to enforce standards throughout the area. Although control has now passed from the Comissão de Viticultura Região de Colares to the Junta Nacional do Vinho, the shaded *adega* in the centre of Colares, with its low white façade and blue and white tiles, still continues to play a central role in the making of the wines, as will appear.

Besides Colares itself, the demarcated region includes the smaller districts of S. João das Lampas and S. Marinho just to the north. What makes the area unique is that the vines are planted in dune sands. Tertiary and Quaternary in origin, they cover a layer of Mesozoic clay to a depth of between 3 and 10 metres. Before the vines can be planted, a wide trench must be dug down to the level of the clay, and the root is then sunk into a hole made with an iron bar. The sides of the trench are liable to collapse without warning; and the man at the bottom habitually works with a basket over his head in case of emergencies and so to avoid suffocation. It would be altogether too laborious, even in Colares, to plant the young vines separately, so that lateral shoots are encouraged to put out subsidiary roots, the sand being replaced in stages to cover them. The mother vine may 'creep' in this way for up to 10 metres, giving rise to what are to all appearances individual plants. The only other parts of Portugal where this method is employed is in small plots in the dune area of the Minho.

If this was not labour enough, the vines must further be protected from the prevailing winds, which sweep in from the Atlantic and would otherwise tear off the leaves and blight the plants with sea-salt. Palisades of cane, woven together with willow, are therefore erected. The higher barricades run parallel to the coast and are bounded at right angles with lower ones or with dry stone walls, so giving the vineyard the appearance of a huge chequerboard. The vines are encouraged to creep low along the ground, and planted among them for further protection are wild roses or plants such as potatoes, the whole untidy ensemble looking like an overgrown rose garden.

The originators of this novel form of viticulture cannot have

Creeping vines at Colares, grown in dune sand and protected from the sea winds by palisades and other vegetation. (Jan Read)

foreseen that in the 1870s and 1880s it would protect their vines against the scourge of phylloxera, which ravaged the rest of Portugal and Europe. That the Ramisco vines, typical of the region, have survived in their native form and need not be grafted is because the insect responsible for the disease cannot penetrate the thick bed of sand.

Apart from the predominant *chão de areia* (sandy soil), there are smaller areas of *chão rijo* (firm soil) producing a much inferior wine. At one time this was blended with the true Colares, but the practice is now forbidden.

All authentic Colares must be made by the Adega Regional; and the practice is for the large *négociants* (of whom there are now only four) to deliver their grapes to it for vinification. In return they receive the equivalent amount of wine and a sufficient number of *selos de origem* to cover its bottling after the wine has been matured in their own *adegas*. Wine made from grapes supplied by small farmers is matured in the Adega Regional and sold under its own label.

The wine is vinified at the Adega by passing the grapes through a crusher into open cement tanks, where the first fermentation proceeds for two or three days, the solid matter being submerged manually with a wooden *macaco*. The wine is then run off the *bagaço* (or *marc*) into wooden *toneis*, in which fermentation continues more slowly for about another month. In March the wine is racked into fresh casks and after maturing for an obligatory two years becomes limpid and dark ruby in colour.

In practice, red Colares, averaging some 11° to 12° of alcohol, is astringent and rich in tannin and requires long years in cask and bottle if it is to emerge at its glorious best—much of it disappoints because it is drunk far too young. One of the most scrupulous of the producers is António Bernardino Paulo da Silva, a bubbling enthusiast of a man, who, despite rocketing labour costs, continues to cultivate his vines in traditional fashion and to age his wines for long years in the oak and chestnut casks of his *adega* overlooking the Atlantic. As a result, his 'Colares Chita' regularly wins gold medals in the Concurso Nacional organized by the Junta Nacional do Vinho.

P. Morton Shand once likened the flavour of mature Colares to that of 'one of the fuller Beaujolais, such as Juliénas'. My own tasting notes on the 1968 red 'Colares Chita', which had spent ten years in wood and three in bottle, were: 'dark ruby colour, aromatic and very healthy nose, fruity and extraordinarily young in taste for such an old wine, still astringent with a long and individual finish. A very good wine.' An even older wine, the Casal de Azenha 1957, was a dark ruby red with orange rim and ripe fruity nose, very full and silky with a rich flavour of mature fruit, long finish and only a hint of astringency at the end—a fine example of red Colares at its glorious best.

Of the white Colares, Shand wrote that it 'is not so much a poor as a positively nasty wine'. While the whites are clearly not in the same class as the reds, I would not go so far. The 1968 'Chita', made from a blend of Arinto, Malvasia and Dona Branca grapes, was a brilliant pale greenish straw colour, faintly perfumed, without much fruit and with a hint of sulphur, and dry to a degree with astringent finish.

The average annual production of Colares has tended to fall and stands at about 2300 hectolitres.

SETÚBAL

The fourth of the demarcated regions in the Lisbon area lies south across the great suspension bridge and around the port of Setúbal, now in the throes of industrial expansion, from which it takes its name. Apart from the famous Moscatel, the Setúbal Peninsula, with its rocky coastline and charming seaside resorts of Sesimbra and Portinho, produces large amounts of very drinkable red wine (see Chapter 9).

Although there is no record of Moscatel de Setúbal as such until the nineteenth century, the area has been known for its wines since the Phoenicians founded the little port of Cetóbriga (present-day Setúbal) and the Romans later developed the vineyards. Various authors have conjectured that the legendary 'Osey', drunk both in England and by the King of Hungary in the fourteenth century, originated here. Professor Roger Dion, in his scholarly *Histoire de la Vigne et du Vin en France*, derives the name from 'Azoia', still used of the coastal strip between the mouths of the Tagus and Sado rivers. There is an intriguing reference to Setúbal, probably a sweet fortified wine, since it is listed between Madeira and Muscat de Toulon, in the accounts of an auction of the Duc d'Aiguillon's cellar in 1793, reproduced in Pierre Vital's *Les Vielles Vignes de notre France*. It is of interest that it fetched 5 livres a bottle, whereas Margaux went for only 1 livre 16 sols.

The little town of Azeitão had become the wine centre of the region as early as the mid-eighteenth century, since a contemporary writer, Joaquim Gomes de Oliveira, informs us that in 1759 'because of the quality of its soil and its advantageous situation for making good wines, Azeitão is known today, as it has been in the past, for the most interesting wines and best cultivated vineyards in the region'. It was at Azeitão in 1834 that José Maria Fonseca founded the well-known firm of the same name,

71

perfecting the Moscatel de Setúbal, which since 1849 has won no less than 191 gold and silver medals at international exhibitions, including a gold medal at the most famous of all, the Paris Universal Exhibition of 1889, for which the Eiffel Tower was built.

The region was demarcated in 1907, and its 60,000 hectares included large areas of sandy soil no longer used for growing Moscatel. Official statistics for the production of the wine (p. 171) are therefore somewhat confusing because they include the red table wine now grown on these soils. The position is under review, and it seems likely that a reduced area of some 10,000 hectares will be demarcated for Moscatel de Setúbal and that a new region producing red wines of the 'Periquita' type will also be defined. It has further been proposed that the wine made in the newly demarcated Moscatel region should be called 'Setúbal' *tout court*, and not 'Moscatel de Setúbal'.

After the original demarcation in 1907, later decrees defined grape varieties, methods of viticulture and commercial procedures; and in 1934 control was vested in the União Vinícola Regional de Moscatel de Setúbal, whose first Director was António Porto Soares Franco, head of the firm of J. M. da Fonseca and author of the authoritative booklet *O Moscatel de Setúbal*. Under a recent reorganization, the region is now administered by the Junta Nacional do Vinho.

The Moscatel grapes were originally grown on the chalky soil of the valley and the slopes of the sunny Arrábida hills between Azeitão and the Atlantic. During the phylloxera epidemic of the late nineteenth century, the vines were grafted on to stocks of the American *Riparia* and its hybrids and replanted in sandy soil, further inland near Palmela. This did not prove as suitable, and the vines are once again being grown on the northern slopes of the Arrábida hills, the Palmela area being replanted with the black Periquita, which, like the Ramisco in Colares, thrives in the sand without the need for grafting.

The wines are made from two types of Moscatel grape. The preponderant variety, the Moscatel do Setúbal, known as the Alexandria in France and Italy and the Moscatel de Málaga in Spain, grows in large clusters with big berries, thin-skinned and luscious, and changing in colour from green to yellow-amber. A small amount of wine is also made from the black Moscatel Roxo, with smaller clusters and berries, grown on only 2 hectares of vineyards.

Although there are some 900 small farmers growing Moscatel grapes and some 10 per cent of the wine is made in the Adega Cooperativa de Palmela, by far the most important source, both as regards quality and quantity, is J. M. da Fonseca.

The must is vinified in cement vats, and fermentation is checked by the addition of grape spirit when the Baumé degree stands at 5°—sulphur dioxide is never used, as it spoils the taste of Moscatel wines. After vinification the must is transferred to 12,000-litre cement *depósitos*, and lightly crushed grapes and skins are steeped in it, thus producing the marvellously fresh taste of dessert grapes so typical of the wine. In February the wine undergoes its one and only pressing and is then left in large containers for another year before being filtered and passed to casks of some 600 to 650 litres, where it remains until it is bottled. It is racked once a year— though in recent years racking has been more irregular because of shortage of labour—and periodically topped up with wine of the same year to make good the loss by evaporation, which is high. There is no bottle-ageing. During this process, and because of the concentration of sugar by evaporation of the liquid, the degree Baumé increases from 5° to 20° over the decades, and the alcohol content from 18° to 20°, so that the wines end up with the same alcoholic and Baumé degree.

The two types of wine most frequently met with are the six-year-old, with its extraordinary taste of fresh grapes, and the twenty-five-year-old, darker in colour, with a smoother, more honey-like flavour. There is also a Moscatel Roxo, made exclusively from black grapes in very small amount and not obtainable outside Portugal.

These three wines are, however, only the tip of the iceberg; and in the cellars of the Old Winery at Azeitão there are wines known as 'Torna-Viagem'—from being shipped across the equator and back in the manner of Madeira—which are a century and more old.

During a recent visit to Azeitão, I was invited by D. Fernando Porto Soares Franco, the present head of the firm and a direct descendant of José Maria Fonseca, to take part in an extraordinary tasting of his Moscatel, ranging from the youngest to a Torna-Viagem *hors d'âge*. The tasting took place in the cellar and the wines, with ten-year intervals in age between them, were drawn straight from the barrel. As will appear from the accompanying notes, the character of the wine changes progressively with time, and there is a whole gamut of colour, nose and flavour.

1978   Light amber. Strong grapey nose and flavour. Fruity aftertaste. The brandy had not quite amalgamated, and the wine was still a little turbid.

1968   The wine was now bright, with a colour resembling that of *oloroso* sherry. Soft and very fruity, still with a slight taste of brandy and some oak in the nose.

1958   Clear dark brown. Nose like *oloroso* sherry, but completely different in flavour. Smooth, rich and soft with a hint of burnt sugar. Sweet, grapey aftertaste.

1948   The *oloroso* nose was not so marked, and the finish was a little drier.

1938   The colour was significantly darker, though still brown. Beautiful muscat-burnt-sugar nose. Very smooth and sweet right through.

1928   Maderized nose. Very sweet. It tasted to me like cherries and caramel.

At this point in the tasting there was a marked change in colour, perhaps because of a difference in the method of vinification, and the remaining wines were almost black.

1918   Elegant maderized nose, like an old and very rich vintage port. An extraordinary wine and probably the best of the older, with its intense and lingering finish.

1908   Maderized and intensely sweet. Lingering Moscatel finish. Oaky. Prefer the 1918.

1900   Nose not as pronounced. Nutty—burnt-sugar flavour. Slightly drier finish.

TV   A wine which had been shipped to and from the tropics in the manner of Madeira. Pitch black and 'chewy'. The nose was not so much maderized as perfumed, and it tasted like an unctuous cherry liqueur.

After this systematic tasting, we tried a few others.

Roxo 1969   Dark colour. A hint of *oloroso* in the nose. Intensely fruity finish.

Apart from the 1918, which I had so much liked myself, Snhr. Franco regarded the 1927 and 1955 as the best vintages.

1955   A lighter wine, both in nose, colour and taste. Very grapey.
1927   A very large vintage, now finished. Extremely round and honey-like. Nose not as pronounced as some and lighter on the palate than most.

To sum up, the wines reminded me more of old Málagas than any others. This is hardly surprising, since they are made from the same grape; but they are characterized by their intense grapiness, no doubt resulting from the steeping of the skins in the new wine.

Not so long ago it seemed that, because of a prejudice against sweet dessert wines, the production of Moscatel de Setúbal was on the decline. However, demand in Portugal itself, the largest market, has increased. Exports, too, have picked up, and figures (in litres) for the last four years are: 1977, 7422; 1978, 9342; 1979, 12,335; and 1980, 17,424. The best foreign market was traditionally Brazil, where sales of the wine, most of it shipped in cask, ran to about a quarter of those for Port during the 1930s. More recently, the largest foreign markets—though the quantities involved are small—have been the United States, Britain, Canada, Holland and West Germany.

5

Vinhos Verdes or Green Wines

Apart from Port and Madeira, the *vinhos verdes* or Green Wines are Portugal's most individual; and, in fact, nothing like them is to be found elsewhere, except for the pétillant wines from the neighbouring regions of Galicia, grown and made in generally similar fashion, which have not, however, achieved the same renown outside their own immediate area.

Green Wine does not refer to the colour of the wine, but to its youth and freshness. The wines may be either white or red and are made to be drunk young, usually in the spring or summer following the harvest. What distinguishes them from other young wines, which are often only harsh and immature, is their light sparkle and delicacy, resulting from a traditional method of vinification appropriate to a highly individual style of viticulture.

The vines climb high from the ground; the grapes therefore receive less reflected sunshine than those grown on normal low vines and consequently contain less sugar and more of the malic acid found in unripe fruit generally. The bulk of this acid does not, however, persist in the finished wine, but subsequent to the ordinary alcoholic fermentation is broken down by naturally occurring bacteria with the evolution of carbon dioxide gas. This secondary or malo-lactic fermentation is common to all wines, but is ordinarily completed under conditions allowing for the escape of the gas; the *pétillant* quality so delightful in a *vinho verde* would be disastrous, for example, in a red Burgundy. In the early days Champagne was made by just this method—and even drunk from the barrel—until methods were devised for producing a longer-lasting and more pronounced sparkle.

The *vinho verde* produced by a multitude of small proprietors continues to be made by this traditional method—be it noted that,

76

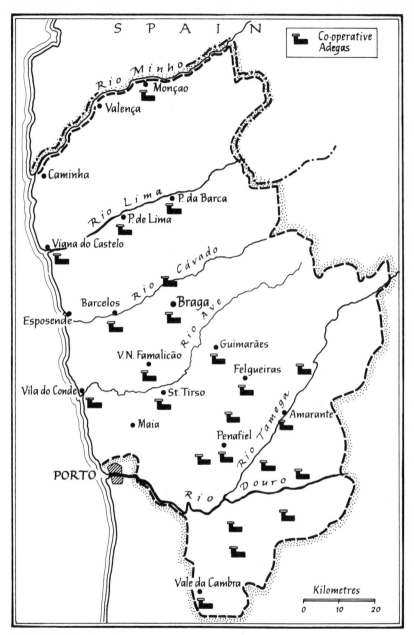

The Vinho Verde region

since the grapes, especially in the south of the region, are sometimes fully ripe when picked, many cooperatives and larger producers often curtail malo-lactic fermentation by using sulphur dioxide and add a little carbon dioxide at a later stage to achieve the characteristic prickle. This has been made a burning issue by journalists and will be discussed more fully later.

The net result of the procedures used for *vinhos verdes* is a wine relatively low in alcohol, possessing a slight impermanent sparkle or *pétillance* and, if properly made, not unduly acid, apart from an astringency derived from the granitic soil on which the vines are grown. At their best the white *vinhos verdes*, actually pale yellow in colour, are wonderfully light and fresh, and the delicate taste of fruit can be more marked than in a wine with a high sparkle like Champagne. They make ideal drinking for hot summer days, especially if one is lucky enough to taste them with the shellfish from the adjacent coast, and, like Champagne, are a pleasant alternative to stronger liquors before a meal.

Although the red wines are not much seen abroad, they constitute 70 per cent of production and are much appreciated in Portugal, where they go well with dishes such as grilled sardines and the rich *ranchos* (or stews); but people coming new to them would agree with Raymond Postgate's assessment—that the 'taste is unrelentingly hard, and the first mouthful is a shock'. He was certainly right in recommending that they should be drunk stone-cold.

Geography and climate

The demarcated region, comprising 823,034 hectares, of which 24,927 hectares are under vines, extends from the Minho River on the Galician border in the north to just south of the Douro. It is bounded by the Atlantic to the west and by the Port region on its eastern extremity. Six sub-regions, different in micro-climate and the quality of their wines, were defined as long ago as 1908 and have recently been recognized by the EEC Commission. These are Monção to the north, and, continuing towards the south, Lima, Braga, Penafiel, Basto and Amarante.

Scenically, this hilly, well-wooded area is one of the most beautiful in Portugal; chestnut and oak trees abound, interspersed as elsewhere in the north with pines and aromatic groves of eucalyptus; the country roads are banked with wild roses and hydrangea; and the vines, a fresh green in spring and a symphony of russets and oranges in autumn, are everywhere in evidence among the other crops, climbing high into the trees, trained between cross-shaped *cruzetas*, or forming shady arbours supported by granite pillars.

The universal presence of granite is the most striking geological feature. It is used almost exclusively for building, for paving, for constructing the dry retaining walls of the terraced hillsides, for hewing pillars to support the vines, and even, in the shape of flat slabs, for fencing. The extensive use of granite was central to the early Minho culture, as is evidenced by the dolmens and monolithic stone figures to be found on either side of the border with Galicia.

Apart from a band of Silurian schists between the lower Lima and Cávado rivers, the soil is almost entirely composed of this granite, broken up either by the action of the weather or by backbreaking toil with the primitive implements available. It is naturally acid in reaction, and the deficiency of lime and phosphorus must be made good with manures.

Rainfall and temperature, though varying across the region from the drier and warmer coastal belt to mountain valleys, which reach a height of almost 700 metres at the eastern extreme, display the same general pattern. The summers, lasting from June until September, are dry and hot, and the winters mild and wet.

Viticulture and grapes

As already mentioned, the landscape resembles nothing so much as a vast and variegated market garden given over to the culture of the high, climbing vine. Of the 80,000 growers, about half are smallholders producing less than two pipes of wine, and only a hundred or so produce more than 100 pipes.

In the most primitive form of culture, the vines, in groups, are simply trained up the trunk and into the foliage of a suitable tree. In the past, the chestnut was the favourite until most of the trees were killed by a fungal blight; no other type has proved quite so successful, though the oak is now commonly used. A modification is to festoon the vines from trunk to trunk along a line of trees bordering a plot used for other crops.

This form of cultivation has many advantages. The grapes are kept well away from the damp ground and are less subject to mildew and parasitic rot, as also to early ground frost in the autumn; the pruning of the trees provides useful fuel; and, while making available space for maize and other crops, the trees with their dependent vines at the same time shelter them from the prevailing Atlantic winds.

The disadvantages are, unfortunately, almost as numerous. The grafts introduced after the damaging phylloxera epidemic of the late nineteenth century are not as suited to climbing as the native vines. The harvesting of the grapes, often a dangerous operation necessitating the employment of long and perilous-looking ladders, calls for devoted and intensive labour, as does the spraying of the vines against mildew and oidium. In the last resort, this factor may well result in the eventual disappearance of the

The grape harvest at the Quinta da Aveleda. (Jan Read)

High-growing vines, grown on cruzetas *in the vineyards of the Casa Compostela near Braga. (Jan Read)*

tree vine, at a time when more and more of the rural population is leaving the land for the higher wages of the cities.

A widespread alternative method of cultivation involves the traditional use of granite pillars, employed either in the form of a *bardo*, in which the vines are trained up wires stretched between rows of uprights, or as supports for a roofed-in arbour. The arbour is more easily accessible, but impedes the culture of the subsidiary crop growing beneath it.

A method increasingly favoured by the larger producers is to train the vines on wires strung between T-shaped uprights of wood or concrete, known as *cruzetas*. The yield may be increased by adding a vertical member at the top and using three wires. The use of *cruzetas* is more practical than the growing of vines on trees, since there is more uniform exposure of the grapes to the sun; they may be picked without ladders; and tractors may be used for the various agricultural operations during the year. Pruning has not yet been mechanized, but may be speeded by the use of pneumatic scissors.

Terracing is widely practised in the Green Wine area, as also in Galicia and the Port region of the Upper Douro, so as to make the fullest use of the hilly terrain. The retaining walls are usually of dry stone masonry of the sort used by the Homeric Greeks. It is a

81

form of agriculture feasible only as a result of land hunger and the availability of cheap labour. The terraces are often so steep as to be inaccessible to tractors and are part and parcel of a system of farming dependent upon animals, which additionally provide manure to enrich the soil. In present circumstances it seems unlikely that they can be maintained on their present scale, let alone extended.

There are four types of black grape widely used in the region as a whole: Azal, Borraçal, Padeiro and Vinhão. The most commonly occurring white grapes are the Azal branco, Esganoso, Loureiro, Pedernã, Rabigate and Trajadura. Other varieties are listed under the individual sub-regions and detailed descriptions are to be found in *Le Vin 'Verde'*, published by the Comissão de Viticultura da Região dos Vinhos Verdes, or in the magnificently illustrated volume *O Portugal Vinícola* (printed with an accompanying French translation) by B.C. Cincinnato da Costa. It may be noted that the Loureiro and Trajadura (Treixadura) are also common in Galicia. Only two of the sub-regions produce a wine made from a single grape variety. Monção is famous for its Alvarinho (known in Galicia as Albariño); and in the lower Lima valley there are red wines made exclusively from the Vinhão. The Vinhão is the one grape to be found in all the sub-regions and is used to give red wines body and strength.

A variety of phylloxera-resistant stocks is employed for grafting; but pure American varieties are rarely used now, with the exception of the *Riparia Gloire de Montpellier*. Hybrids of *Rupestris* are more common; however, the favourite is a hybrid of unknown origin locally known as the Corriola, an unusually vigorous vine well suited to the individual methods of the region.

Government control

The region was demarcated in 1908 by a law which also defined the characteristics of *vinho verde* and the types of grapes and methods of viticulture appropriate to making it. The official regulatory body, the Comissão de Viticultura da Região dos Vinhos Verdes, was formed in 1929 and still operates as an autonymous organization.

It operates from a large building in Oporto, which houses offices and laboratories, both for the routine analysis of samples and also for fundamental research and the bulk production of the specialized yeasts issued to the cooperatives and independent producers. An impressive feature is the *cadastro* or archive, with aerial photographs on file of each and every vineyard in the region—a safeguard against their planting or replanting with unapproved types of vine.

In his book, *Le Vin 'Verde'*, D. Armândio Barbedo Galhano, for long the technical director of the Comissão, describes its functions and legal obligations in great detail. Chief among them are to ensure the continued production of *vinhos verdes* in traditional fashion by the cultivation of high-growing vines and appropriate vinification of their grapes; to prohibit the introduction of grapes or wines from outside the region; and to issue guarantees of origin.

These are distributed to the producers in appropriate number only after the wines have passed strict analytical tests in the Comissão's laboratories and have met with the approval of its expert tasters. As in the other demarcated regions, they take the form of a narrow, numbered paper strip, the *selo de origem*, affixed to the cork and neck of the bottle before capsuling.

Among further important activities in the field, the Comissão draws up architect's plans for new cooperative wineries, underwriting loans for their construction, and offers technical assistance to the producers on a day-to-day basis. Its staff of some 250 is large, as befits the size of a region producing some 25 per cent of all Portuguese wine.

Associated with the Comissão are twenty-one cooperative wineries regularly calling on it for advice, of which the largest at Felgueiras has a capacity of 3 million litres and the smallest at Monção, of 600,000. The farmers or *associados*, who supply grapes to these cooperatives and are paid on the basis of weight and sugar content, elect their own committees and manager in charge of day-to-day operations, so that the cooperatives are not directly controlled by the Comissão. Thirteen of them have formed a large *união* to blend, bottle and market their wine—under the name of 'Vercoope' (from *'verde'* and *'cooperativa'*)—and also to supply them with disease-free stocks from Montpelier, grafted with native varieties of tree-growing vine; and the Comissão itself maintains a warehouse at Maia, outside Oporto, with a capacity for the cold storage of 6 million litres of wine produced in excess of current demand. It also operates three large distilleries for converting unsold wine (mostly red) into grape spirit, made, like grain whisky, by the continuous process. This is sold to AGE (Administración Geral de Alcool), which disposes of it to private firms for elaboration as brandy or to the port companies for brandying their wine.

Harvesting

Autumn is a period of exceptional activity in the Green Wine Area with its many different crops, since it is not only the grapes, but also the haricot beans and maize, which must be harvested. The date is usually fixed by rule of thumb, though the Comissão and the cooperatives are trying to introduce more rational methods based on the density and acid content of the grape juice. It is the rule for harvesting to start early rather than late; and once under way, all the grapes are picked at the same time, the black immediately after the white. Traditionally, the fruit is first gathered into baskets and then transferred to panniers of sufficient capacity to produce an *almude* (or 25 litres) of wine.

It is a most picturesque ceremony. On the large estates the pickers range from old women in black (in Spain and Portugal half the senior population is in mourning for aunts and second cousins) to students in jeans and sneakers and black-haired lively-eyed girls in colourful sweaters and gum boots. Many carry umbrellas as protection against the lurking rainstorms; and at the end of the day, when they return Indian file down the narrow lanes between the vines, each with a basket and tapering ladder, they look like nothing so much as Walt Disney's gnomes on their homeward trek. And while they pick they sing. António Guedes at Aveleda once told me that his grandfather was always glad when he heard the pickers singing, because it meant that they were not eating the grapes!

Vinification

The whole traditional technique of making *vinhos verdes* turns around the eventual elimination of malic acid, present in the must in quantities of up to 15 g/litre, which would otherwise render the wine unacceptably sharp and acid. In the past—and even today in the tiny village *adegas*—the grapes were pressed in open stone

The end of the day. Grape harvesters returning from the vineyards of the Quinta da Aveleda. (Jan Read)

troughs and matured in wooden casks until the following spring, total reliance being placed on the naturally occurring yeasts and bacterias to bring about the desired transformation.

In its periodic *Estudos, Notas e Relatórios*, the Comissão has reported on researches carried out in its laboratories which have thrown a great deal of light on the processes involved in the time-established method. The first is a normal fermentation in which the grape sugar is broken down into alcohol. It is not, however, the carbon dioxide generated at this point which gives the wine its

85

slight sparkle. In the presence of the lees at the bottom of the barrel, the original yeasts break down and bacteria known as *Leuconostoc* and *Lactobacillus* appear, which, some months after the original fermentation, induce the secondary so-called malo-lactic fermentation. Under proper conditions the malic acid is almost entirely converted into the less harsh and smoother-tasting lactic acid, with the simultaneous production of small amounts of carbon dioxide.

The whole cycle operates most effectively if the original fermentation is carried out at relatively low temperatures and small amounts of sulphur dioxide are added to inhibit the growth of organisms inimical to the *Lactobacillus*. Premature racking (or decanting of the wine from the lees) can also interfere with the secondary fermentation. As a result of its experimental work the Comissão has produced and distributes a preparation of selected strains of yeasts and bacillus which produces optimum results.

The red *vinhos verdes* are fermented in contact, not only with the skins and pips, but also with the stalks. This can only result in high tannin content and no doubt contributes to the uncompromising character of wines already drier and more acid than most.

The whites are made *en blanc* or *bica aberta*, all of the skins and pips, and also, of course, the stalks, being removed before fermentation.

The wines are not frequently racked—though this is always done in November when they 'fall bright'—because, as already explained, it interferes with secondary fermentation. Normally they clarify without difficulty, especially when, as recommended by the Comissão, bentonite is added to the must before fermentation. A month or two later they are already markedly *pétillant*, less acid and smoother, thanks to the breakdown of malic acid. When ready for drinking they contain 8° to 11·5° of alcohol. The white wines from Monção differ from the others in containing some 12° to 14°; and the producers were in fact penalized on this account, having to pay fines to the government, until the exceptional qualities of the growth were officially recognized in 1951.

Typical figures for the composition of a *vinho verde* made in this fashion, before and after malo-lactic fermentation, are given below:

	Wine immediately after alcoholic fermentation	Wine with malo-lactic fermentation in progress
Density at 15°C	1·000	0·9996
Percent alcohol by volume	9·65	9·80
Dry extract (g/litre)	31·52	27·84
Volatile acid (g/litre) (expressed as sulphuric)	0·36	0·66
Volatile acid (g/litre) (expressed as acetic)	0·44	0·80
Fixed acid (g/litre) (expressed as sulphuric)	7·48	4·07
Fixed acid (g/litre) (expressed as tartaric)	11·45	7·62
Ash (g/litre)	3·53	3·03
Tartaric acid (g/litre)	4·26	3·18
Malic acid (g/litre)	6·39	2·79
Lactic acid (g/litre)	0·7	3·49
Reducing sugar (g/litre)	1·32	0·0

Most of the wine which is bottled and sold commercially is now made in the lined concrete vats of the cooperatives, under instructions from the oenologists of the Comissão, or in the modern equipment of the large private firms, which includes stainless steel tanks. This has led to the employment of new and modified methods of vinification.

In the past, secondary fermentation took place in closed barrels, so that all of the carbon dioxide was retained in the wine, which was drunk from the wood in the manner of farmhouse cider. In the small bars of the Minho it is still possible to obtain *vinho verde* drawn from the cask—and very delicious it is. However, increasingly more of the smallholders now take their grapes to the cooperatives to be vinified. In their open cement vats, the free carbon dioxide bubbles off—though, of course, a certain amount remains dissolved in the wine—and with the commercialization of *vinho verde* in bottles, it was obviously desirable to market a stable product and to avoid bursts and exploding corks.

At the same time, it is very noticeable that in a good year the grapes grown on the *cruzetas* of the newer vineyards are sweet and

Modern stainless steel fermentation vats at the Casa Compostela.
(Jan Read)

fully ripened, and a special malo-lactic fermentation hardly seems necessary. In the larger, modern establishments it has therefore become the practice to cool the wine and to add a little carbon dioxide from cylinders to give it the slight *pétillance* which would otherwise be lacking.

On a recent visit to José Maria da Fonseca, I asked the skilled oenologist, D. João Pedro Miller Guerra about the methods used for making Lancers *vinho verde*, produced in the very south of the area at Baião and Cinfães. His comments were most illuminating.

Since the grapes are normally quite ripe when picked, there is no need for a special malo-lactic fermentation, and sulphur dioxide is added in small amount to prevent it. The wine is neither sweetened nor aerated with carbon dioxide, and the only additament is a little ascorbic acid used as an anti-oxidant. Asked about extended malo-lactic fermentation generally, Snhr. Guerra said that it was not strictly necessary in good years when the acid content of the fruit was low and the sugar content high. It reduces the fruitiness of the wine, but is still often practised as a matter of routine, because it is a tradition and the growers and smaller cooperatives do not possess the skill to curtail it by adding sulphur dioxide in the correct amount, and also because its delayed occurrence in bottles may lead to bursts.

There is no standard way of making the wines in the bigger concerns. Another factor which has led to modifications is that, with growing exports, foreign consumers have asked for sweeter wines. *Vinho verde* is bone-dry in its natural state, and sweeter wines may be made either, as with the popular 'Aveleda', by removal of the yeasts by centrifugation or addition of sulphur dioxide before fermentation is complete; or, if a still sweeter wine is required, by blending a sweet must, as in the case of 'Gatão' from Borges & Irmão. Again, the use of stainless steel tanks has made possible 'cold' fermentation and the retention of more of the fruit in the nose and flavour: an outstanding example is the beautiful 'Palacio de Brejoeira' made exclusively from Alvarinho grapes fermented at 18°C.

Sub-regions of the Vinho Verde

It is frequently not possible to tell by the label from which of the sub-regions a particular *vinho verde* originates. Those, for example, from Vercoope are a blend of wines from thirteen widely scattered cooperatives; on the other hand, the wines from the cooperatives at Ponte de Lima and Monção are definitely *sui generis* and of the sub-region, as are those from a variety of private concerns such as the Sociedade Agricola da Quinta da Aveleda, the Quinta de San Claudio, the Casa Compostela and the Palacio de Brejoeira.

The distinctions between wines produced in the different areas result both from the micro-climate and predominant variety of grape. Only in the sub-regions of Penafiel and Amarante do the white wines for which the region is best-known abroad account for as much as 30 per cent of total production. The smaller districts of Celorico de Basto and Santa Tirso make about 20 per cent and 15 per cent of white wine respectively, and the rest of the demarcated regions 5 per cent or less.

MONÇÃO (Black grapes: Vinhão or Negrão, Cainhos, Doçar, Brancelho. White grapes: Alvarinho and Loureiro.)

There is general agreement that the best wine of the whole demarcated region is the white Alvarinho from Monção; but in the Minho opinions differ as to whether it can be described as

The Adega Cooperativa de Felgueiras, typical of the many modern cooperative wineries in the Vinho Verde region. (Comissão de Viticultura da Região dos Vinhos Verdes)

completely 'green'. Owing to its higher alcohol content and lower than average effervescence, in Portuguese eyes it is half-way towards a *vinho maduro*, and like the Albariño from Galicia is sometimes compared with Moselle. Because of the scarcity of Alvarinho grapes and low yield of must (they are thick-skinned with numerous pips) production amounts to only 2 per cent of the total for the sub-region as a whole and the wines are correspondingly expensive.

There are only three commercial producers of Alvarinho. The Adega Cooperativa Regional de Monção, numbering 378 *associados*, makes its wines in lined concrete vats. Of its annual production of 600,000 litres, only 20,000 bottles emerge as an excellent white Alvarinho, fragrant and fruity.

The winery and cellars of Vinhos de Monção Lda. occupy old-fashioned premises in a lane on the outskirts of this picturesque old town overlooking the broad Minho River and the wooded shore of Galicia on the opposite bank. The *adega* proper lies up a narrow flight of steps from the small office and is strictly limited in size, because expansion would be profitless in view of the difficulty in obtaining more Alvarinho grapes of sufficient quality in competition with the cooperative. All of the wine is fermented in

90

wood and matured in chestnut barrels, and total production, including a red wine and a *bagaceira* as well as the famous white 'Cépa Velha', amounts to 50,000 litres—which leaves little scope for export.

In recent years, the 'Cépa Velha', which has won dozens of medals in international exhibitions, has been somewhat over-shadowed by the wine from the Palacio de Brejoeira, with its 17 hectares of vineyards planted exclusively with Alvarinho. The winery adjoins an impressive Manueline-style mansion outside Monção and is equipped with modern horizontal presses and stainless steel tanks, hosed down or moistened with damp cloths to allow for 'cold' fermentation. Under the expert supervision of D. Amândio Barbado Galhano, formerly the technical director of the Comissão, Brejoeira is producing sizeable quantities of a first-rate Alvarinho, very pale, fragrant and elegant, and fruity and dry right through. It is an expensive wine, but has been likened to a good Chenin blanc.

THE BASTO (Black grapes: Vinhão, Espadeiro de Basto, Boraçal, Azal tinto. White grapes: Azal branco and Pedernã.)

The Manueline Palace of Brejoeira outside Monção. Its owners make one of the most select Alvarinho wines. (Jan Read)

91

The best of the wines from this sub-region, which centres on the valley of the River Tâmega, are from Celorico de Basto, situated at between 240 and 270 metres. The vines, growing to heights of 9 or 12 metres, form dense curtains between the trees at the roadside and yield wines containing some 9° of alcohol and rather less effervescence than is usual. Basto-type wines account for about 6 per cent of all Green Wines.

AMARANTE (Black grapes: Vinhão or Tinto Nacional, Boraçal, Azal tinto and Espadeiro. White grape: Azal branco.)

The wines from this sub-region are also highly regarded by the Portuguese. Lower in altitude than the Basto and bordering the Douro River, it produces rather heavier and stronger wines, the reds being noted for their deep colour.

BRAGA (Black grapes: Vinhão or Tinto, Borraçal, Espadeiro and Azal tinto. White grapes: Dourado and Azal branco.)

The district takes its name from the ancient city of Braga, famous for its Roman remains, medieval walls and splendid Gothic cathedral. If there is no argument about the general superiority of the 'green' wines from Monção, the Basto and Amarante, Braga is recognized as producing a representative wine, agreeably sharp and effervescent.

There are several good private *adegas* in the sub-region, producing wine of marked quality and individuality. The oldest, the Quinta de São Claudio, is a small estate in the mountains back from the coast near Esposende, owned by Snhr. Costa Leme, a former President of the Comissão. Its 4 hectares, planted entirely with the white Loureiro, produce only 20 pipes of wine (of 500 litres each) annually. The wine, made in oak casks, is a pale lemon yellow, with delicate flowery nose and somewhat astringent finish.

The Casa Compostela near Farmalicão, founded by a wealthy textile manufacturer in 1974, owns a sizeable 28 hectares of vineyards planted with the white Pedernã, Trajadura, Loureiro and Azal. The modern *adega* is equipped with horizontal presses and stainless steel fermentation tanks and produces some 800 pipes of an elegant, pale-coloured wine, light and gentle, with a flowery bouquet and subdued bubble. The Quinta das Bouças near Braga is the venture of another business magnate with romantic

The modern adega *of the Casa Compostela.* (*Jan Read*)

feelings for his native countryside. D. Albano de Castro e Sousa began by replanting the vineyards with Loureiro and Trajadura vines and again uses modern horizontal presses and stainless steel vats. Output has increased from 7000 litres in 1974 to 75,000 litres in 1979, and his wines are exceptionally fresh and fruity with a lingering finish.

PENAFIEL (Black grapes: Vinhão, Borraçal, Espadeiro, Azal tinto. White grapes: Azal branco, Esganoso, Murrão, Cascal.)

In terms of production, Penafiel is second only to Braga, contributing about a fifth of the total of Green Wine. Among the knowledgeable there is some disagreement over its quality, the consensus of opinion being that the wines are somewhat superior to those from Braga and not quite the equal of those from Amarante, which they generally resemble.

The most famous estate is the Quinta da Aveleda, which must be one of the most beautifully sited wineries in Portugal—or the world. The surrounding gardens, sheltered by pines, oak and eucalyptus, are ablaze in spring with rhododendrons, azaleas and blue and pink hydrangeas. The old house and winery, connected

93

At the Quinta da Aveleda. (Jan Read)

by trellised arbours of vine, give directly on to a more formal garden with fountains and pools carpeted with water lily.

The estate belongs to the Guedes family, who also control the Sociedade Comercial dos Vinhos de Mesa de Portugal (SOGRAPE), makers of 'Mateus Rosé', and the Vinícola do Vale do Dão, producers of the popular 'Grão Vasco', thus making them the biggest wine concern in the country. In 1860, D. Manuel Pedro Guedes da Silva Fonseca began planting vineyards in the French style, with different varieties of vine on separate plots. This obviously allows for more sophistication in the making of the wine than is possible at a cooperative, which contracts to receive grapes of assorted varieties from its members, the only usual distinction being between white and black.

The Quinta da Aveleda grows 10 per cent of the grapes used for its wines and owns 24 hectares of vineyards. The picturesque old buildings of the winery house modern horizontal presses, the familiar lined concrete vats and an up-to-date bottling line. The most stylish of its white wines, the 'Quinta da Aveleda', delicately perfumed and completely dry, is made from only three grapes, mainly from the vineyards of the estate itself: Loureiro, Traja-

94

dura and Pedernã. For the big-selling 'Aveleda' and 'Casal Garcia' (see below), three other grapes may be employed: Azal branco, Avesso and Douradinha (though this is not much favoured).

LIMA (Black grapes: Vinhão, Borraçal, Verdelhos, Espadeiro. White grapes: Dourada, Caínho branco, Branco Lameiro.)

This last of the sub-regions lies along the valley of the Lima River and produces mainly red wine. This has been criticized for lacking the lightness and verve of other *vinhos verdes* and appeals to people who prefer something more approaching a *vinho maduro* (or ordinary mature wine), more fully bodied, deeper in colour, and relatively stronger in alcohol.

I confess that my own favourite among the red *vinhos verdes* is made at the Adega Cooperativa de Ponte de Lima, which uses *automaticos*, or closed vats of the Algerian type (see p. 49), with a water cooling system and a valve at the top allowing for continuous submersion of the 'cap'. In our household we drink it with rich or oily food, such as haggis or kippers—though I doubt whether it will ever be a serious rival to whisky in Scotland!

Leading producers and exports

Apart from the firms with their own installations in the region, such as the Sociedade da Quinta da Aveleda, J. M. da Fonseca and Borges & Irmão, many of the large concerns bottle and market a *vinho verde*, often a blend. In general the Portuguese themselves prefer the traditional bone-dry white wines, but there is a growing market for wines with a little sweetness, such as 'Aveleda', or the definitely sweet, like 'Gatão' from Borges & Irmão. Of the traditional dry white wines with a good 'green' taste, the most frequently encountered in Portugal is 'Casal Garcia' from Aveleda, followed by others such as 'Lagosta' from the Real Companhía Vinícola do Norte de Portugal, 'Gamba' from Borges & Irmão, 'Casa Mendes' from Caves Aliança, 'Casalinho' from Caves do Casalinho and 'Ribeiros' from Ribeiro & Irmão.

Although exports of red *vinho verde* remain fairly steady at around 800,000 litres—by far the largest market being Brazil— shipments of white wine have increased from 2,965,585 litres in 1977 to 4,182,209 litres in 1980. The British in particular are rapidly acquiring a taste for it, and even estate-made wines like the superb Alvarinho from the Palacio de Brejoeira are now available. Wines which scored highly at a *Decanter* tasting held in May 1979 were 'Gatão', 'Aveleda', 'Casaleiro', 'Verdegar' (from the cooperative union of Vercoope) and 'Casalinho'. Two newcomers to the British market, 'Messias' and 'Magrico', are dry, clean and fresh, and excellent value for money—as are, indeed, the *vinhos verdes* as a whole.

The grape harvest at the Quinta das Bouças in the Vinho Verde *area* *near Braga. (Jan Read)*

The neo-Manueline Palace Hotel at Buçaco, famous for its vintage wines. (*Jan Read*)

Aerial view of SOGRAPE's new winery at Anadia in the Bairrada for making 'Mateus Rosé'. (*SOGRAPE*)

6

Dão

Portuguese wine lists usually draw a distinction between two categories of wine: *vinho verde* and *vinho maduro*. This is a logical consequence of the importance of Green Wine, which constitutes about a quarter of Portugal's total production. Of the *vinhos maduros*, made by the methods customary elsewhere, one of the best, and certainly the most plentiful from the demarcated regions, is Dão. It is pronounced something like 'dong'—the Portuguese, even more than the British, regularly 'eat' their words! Only in fairly recent years and because of the re-organization of the industry have the wines begun to make an impact on foreign markets. The better-known is the red, which accounts for 97 per cent of the output; but the region also produces some good white wine, yet to receive due recognition.

The Dão forms an isolated enclave in central Portugal, being shut off by mountains except for a gap to the west near Coimbra. To the east it is bounded by the high plateau extending into Spain, and to the south and north by the Serra da Estrela and the Caramulo mountains. It is well-watered by a network of rivers flowing into the Mondego at the centre, but has taken its name from the lesser Dão River, perhaps because its course lies entirely within the area.

The focus of the region has always been the town of Viseu, the meeting place of at least six Roman roads. The recorded history of the town dates from the eleventh century, when Fernando of León rebuilt the cathedral after reconquering the place from the Moors. With narrow, steeply climbing streets, lined with cavernous shops, it still has an oriental flavour; but today the heart of old Viseu is the wide, granite-paved cathedral square at the top, flanked to the north by the sixteenth-century Três Escalöes

97

The Dão

Palace, now a museum named after the painter, Grão Vasco, a master of the Viseu Primitive School, who has also lent his name to one of the best-known Dão wines. Apart from its earlier remains, the cathedral also contains a graceful Renaissance cloister decorated with the flamboyant blue and white *azulejos* typical of this part of Portugal.

Soil and climate

The demarcated region embraces the districts of Aguiar de Beira, Sátão, Penalva do Castelo, Fornos de Algodres, Viseu (with the exception of five small parishes), Mangualde, Tondela, Nelas, Gouveia, Mortágua, Santa Combo Dão, Carregal do Sal, Tábua, Oliveira do Hospital, Seia and Arganil—in all an area of 376,400

98

hectares or about 1000 square miles. Of this, only about 18,000 hectares or one-twentieth is under vines, compared, for example, with 43,000 in the Rioja. The highest parts of the zone reach 1900 metres, but it is the land lying between 200 and 500 metres, about half of the total, which grows the best grapes.

Pitted by mountains and canyoned by rivers, the region is nevertheless not geologically complex, consisting almost entirely of granite. Of varying degrees of hardness, some of it may be broken up fairly easily for planting; in other instances recourse must be had to blasting. There are smaller areas of schist, not much used for growing black grapes, but sometimes favoured for the cultivation of the white.

The demarcated region is further divided into three sub-regions on the basis of informed opinion on the quality of the grapes there produced. Approximately two-thirds of the land area, constituting the poorer and more mountainous parts, forms a peripheral 'buffer' zone enclosing the better and more productive central districts. This was done to prevent the smuggling of inferior wines into the area from outside, as happened during the eighteenth and nineteenth centuries in the case of the Upper Douro region demarcated for Port. There is, in fact, little to choose between the quality of the wine from the two central zones, respectively north and south of the Mondego River—though buyers consider that some of the best of it comes from Mangualde and Nelas, south of Viseu in the foothills of the Serra da Estrela. It would seem that the quality depends more on the micro-climate, the altitude and slope of the land, and upon grape variety and viticulture generally than on geographical boundaries.

Monthly mean temperature at Viseu during July and August is 18°C and in January, the coldest month, 6°C; but an absolute maximum of 38°C has been recorded in the summer, and temperatures below freezing point during the other eight months of the year. The rapid drop of temperature in the autumn has useful practical application in slowing up the fermentation of the wine.

As in the *Vinho Verde* region, rainfall is low during the summer and relatively high from November until the end of March, with an average of 1000 millimetres per annum.

Viticulture

The summer aspect of the central Dão is of shimmering green vineyards, splashed with dark belts of pine and broken by expanses of naked granite. Terracing is more common in the peripheral mountain zone; and it is only in these outlying areas that the vines are grown high. Elsewhere the vines are planted singly or in the larger, better-managed vineyards in continuous trailing cordons supported by wires and stakes, and in either case do not exceed 60 centimetres in height. The plots are typically small and divided—there are some 40,000 individual growers in the region—and few of them produce as much as 150 hectolitres (approximately 3300 gallons) per 260 hectares.

The most time-consuming and laborious operation is the digging of holes and trenches in the rocky soil, in which to plant the vines.

Vineyards in the Dão near Viseu. (Jan Read)

100

Spraying against mildew and oidium does not present the same problem as with the high-growing vines of the *Vinhos Verdes.*

A profusion of vines is grown; and, in fact, one of the problems that faces the regulatory body, the Federação dos Vinicultores do Dão, is to persuade the smallholders to pull up old and inferior types and to replant with the approved varieties, which are:

Black	*White*
Touriga Nacional	Arinto do Dão (Assario
Alfrocheiro Preto	branco)
Tinta Amarela	Borrado das Moscas (Bical
Tinta Pinheira (Rufete or	da Bairrada)
Penamcor)	Cerceal
Alvarelhão (Pilongo)	Barcelo
Jaen	Encruzado
	Verdelho

Details and photographs of these varieties are to be found in *La Region Délimitée des Vins du 'Dão'* by Virgilio Correia de Loureiro, a study of the region drawn up by the Federação for presentation to the Office International du Vin.

The yield from most of the varieties is low and unpredictable because, as D. Ferreira de Almeida, oenologist to the Federação, has noted in a recent publication, the larger proportion is to a greater or less extent infected by virus. There is therefore an urgent need for clonal selection of resistant varieties. This has been done with excellent results in the case of the Touriga Nacional, and it is now obligatory for the musts used in making red wines to contain not less than 20 per cent of this grape.

In good years the harvest takes place between mid-September and mid-October, and it is traditionally the women who are left with the hard work of picking the grapes and carrying the laden baskets, on their heads, to the presses or waiting trucks.

Government control

As already mentioned (p. 30), protection of Dão wines dates back to the twelfth century. Another example of early protectionism is a somewhat plaintive plea to the municipality of Viseu from the Chevalier Braz do Ameral, who in 1553 sought permission to purchase 35 *almudes* (875 litres) of *vinho maduro* because he could not stomach his own Green Wine. This would seem to indicate that wine-making methods have changed; but it seems probable that until the early years of the present century most of the wine was peasant-made and coarse.

One of the first to recognize the special merits of the region for viticulture was the eminent oenologist Professor Cincinnato da Costa, who suggested as early as 1900 that it should be demarcated. However, it was not until 1908 that this was finally done, and subsequent efforts to improve the wines were sporadic and slow. In 1934 the União Vinícola do Dão was formed; and in 1942 a further change in organization gave birth to the present Federação dos Vinicultores do Dão, which has done so much to improve standards.

It operates from a handsome building in Viseu, which, apart from offices and laboratories, incorporates a large central hall and cellars, where wine is actually matured and bottled on an experimental scale.

Like the Comissão in the *Vinhos Verdes* area, the Federação lends technical assistance to the multiplicity of small farmers and to the cooperatives, where some 50 per cent of the wine is made, and intervenes in the market to buy and store wine in excess of demand.

To obtain the Federação's *selo de origem*, the wines must pass organoleptic tests covering colour, appearance, bouquet, flavour and stability, and also conform to limits for specific gravity, alcoholic degree, content of fixed and volatile acid, etc.

Since the firms which bottle and market the wines may not legally vinify grapes which they have not themselves grown, the practice is for them to buy from the cooperatives or larger private growers and to blend and mature ready-made wine in their own establishments. Only two, J. M. de Fonseca and the Vinícola do Vale do Dão maintain cellars in the region for this purpose; but the provisions of the Federação apply wherever the wine is subsequently handled.

Important among these are that the red wines must be aged for not less than eighteen months (normally two years) before being bottled and must spend at least two months in bottle, while the whites must be matured for not less than ten months before bottling.

Whenever the wine is moved from one locality to another, a document specifying the amount and quality must be obtained from the Federação; and the casks in which it is matured must be officially sealed to prevent adulteration. Further documentation and tests are necessary before permission is given to export wine under a *certificado de origem* (certificate of origin), and the Federação's inspectors have the right to check and taste specimens at any stage, even on the quayside before shipment abroad.

Working with the Federação are two other organizations, the Centro de Estudos Vitivinícolas do Dão, a research body with laboratories in Nelas, and the Serviços de Cadastro da Região dos Vinhos do Dão, which maintains a detailed register of vineyards.

Vinification

In 1949 Snhr. Loureiro could write of the red wine that pressing and fermentation were still carried out in open granite tanks for the first thirty-six or forty-eight hours, the wine then being run off the *bagaço* (or *marc*) and pumped into wooden barrels, where tumultuous fermentation continued more slowly in the cool of a cellar. In cold weather the result was to delay the complete transformation of sugar into alcohol until the following spring, thus promoting the formation of glycerine and giving the wines the smoothness for which they are noted.

Although the smallholders increasingly take their grapes to the

At a small peasant adega in the village of Silgueiros. (Jan Read)

Large oak casks, or toneis, *for maturing red Dão at Casa Santos Lima in Silgueiros. (Jan Read)*

cooperatives for vinification, many of the old *adegas* are still operational. One which I visited in Silgueiros, south-west of Viseu, a cluster of stone-built houses around a narrow cobbled street, was a tiny cellar, its earth floor muddy with wine. It boasted only a granite *lagar*, into which the bunches of grapes, stalks and all, were emptied and trodden by foot, a *depósito* for allowing the wine to settle, and a few casks. The wine was a dark, plummy red with a Moscatel-like nose, fruity with a hint of sweetness in the middle and a dry astringent finish. They had, in fact, used some Moscatel—and it is customary to add a small proportion of white grapes to obtain the ruby colour so much admired in the region.

Outside Silgueiros is a medium-sized private *adega*, that of Casa Santos Lima, making some 500,000 litres of wine annually—which it is permitted to do since the grapes are from its own vineyards. Here the grapes are destalked and mechanically crushed before vinification in cement vats; and its wines are aged in wooden *toneis* (large barrels) for three to six months before being sold to larger concerns for maturation and marketing. The red is fruity and not too astringent, and the white fresh and of good quality—formerly some of it was sold for making sparkling wine, until this was stopped because of a general shortage of white Dão.

Private concerns of this size are the exception rather than the rule, and the Dãos sold under brand labels are in the main blends of wine bought from the cooperatives. Of these, there are now ten sited in the principal areas of production at Ervedal da Beira, Mangualde, Nelas, Nogueira do Cravo, Penalva do Castelo, Santa Combo Dão, São Paio (Gouveia), Tondela, Silgueiros and Vila Nova de Tazem. The smallest, at Ervedal da Beira, has a total capacity of 9280 hectolitres and an average annual output of 2500 hectolitres, and the largest, at Silgueiros, a capacity of 96,380 hectolitres and annual output of 40,000 hectolitres. The combined capacity and average annual output are 405,820 hectolitres and 211,500 hectolitres.

The Mangualde cooperative, typical of the other modern installations, lies on the outskirts of the village of the same name, well worth a visit from any traveller in the district as the seat of the Casa Anadia, one of the most beautiful of the smaller palaces in Portugal. The ancient, spreading, umbrella-like plane tree in its courtyard must be unique; and the blue and white *azulejos*, representing bizarre scenes from a world in which the animals have mastered the humans, the donkey belabouring his owner, a sow savaging a woman or fish swimming in the clouds, are among the finest eighteenth-century ceramics in the country.

The twentieth century's contribution to the local scene, the great concrete cooperative, has a capacity of some 30,000 hectolitres. The *associados* deliver their grapes in the reception area, where they are weighed and proceed by way of destalking and crushing machinery to large concrete vats of the automatic type, providing for continuous submersion of the *manta* (or cap). The white wines are fermented *bica-aberta* (*en blanc*), after removal of the pips and skins. The new wine is subsequently rested in cool underground *depósitos*, from which samples are drawn up in a long-handled cup, like the *venencia* used in the sherry district, for the benefit and approval of the prospective buyers, who make their purchases by January or February.

Red Dão requires several years ageing in wood for its quality to emerge. Since the cooperatives do not keep the wine beyond the spring or summer following the harvest, this takes place at the *adega* of the purchaser. The methods of the Vinícola do Vale do Dão, one of the outposts of the Guedes family, are representative of the large firms generally. On its arrival in Viseu from the various cooperatives, the wine is temporarily stored in large plastic-lined concrete 'balloons' of up to 1820 hectolitres' capacity. They are in fact constructed by a method developed for cheap housing. The igloo style did not catch on, but has become widespread up and down Portugal for making large containers for the storage of wine. The first step is to inflate a huge rubber balloon, which is covered with a network of curving steel rods and then sprayed with concrete. The balloon is subsequently deflated and the interior coated with epoxy resin.

Different consignments of wine from the 'balloons' are blended to achieve the established flavour and style of the wine in question,

The construction of a 'balloon' (at Borges & Irmão, near Oporto) by the spraying of concrete on to a huge inflated rubber balloon reinforced with steel rods. (Jan Read)

The sixteenth-century house of the Conde de Santar, maker of one of the few estate-grown Dãos. (Jan Read)

in this case 'Grão Vasco', and then run into wooden barrels. This part of the winery, with its tiered and serried rows of barrels, more resembles one of the bodegas in the Rioja—though many of the barrels are much larger than the 225-litre *bordelesas*. All the red 'Grão Vasco' is aged in wood for at least three years and for a further period in bottle. The *reservas* differ from the younger wine only in being aged for longer, but gain considerably in the process.

Apart from the occasional wine, like that made from Semillon and Cabernet Sauvignon grapes in the tiny *adega* of the charming Quinta da Insua, a headquarters for Wellington during the Peninsular War, the only estate-made wine available on a commercial scale is from the Conde de Santar.

The estate, belonging to the Santar family, lies between Viseu and Nelas, and at its heart is the long, low sixteenth-century house with balustraded balcony, set in formal gardens with neatly clipped hedges and fountains tiled with blue *azulejos*. All around

107

Fountain in the grounds of the Conde de Santar. (*Jan Read*)

lie the 60 hectares of vineyards, planted with the white Arinto, Fernão Pires and Azal branco grapes, and the red Mortagua, Baga de Louro and Tourigo. The *adega*, adjoining the house and gardens, formerly housed traditional granite *lagares*, but is now equipped with concrete *autovinificadores* and the wines are made and marketed for the family by the large Lisbon firm of Carvalho, Ribeiro & Ferreira. They are first aged at the *adega* in large oak *toneis* of 29,000 litre capacity and later transferred to Carvalho, Ribeiro & Ferreira's cellars near Vila Franca north of Lisbon for further ageing in wood and bottle. The annual production of the Conde de Santar amounts to as much as 600,000 litres in good years.

The analysis which follows is typical of a representative red Dão.

ANALYSIS OF A RED DÃO WINE

Density	0·9936
Alcohol (% by volume)	12·72
Dry extract	27·06 g/litre
Glycerine	12·10 g/litre
pH	3·32
Total acid (expressed as tartaric)	4·41 g/litre
Volatile acid (expressed as acetic)	0·66 g/litre
Fixed acid (expressed as tartaric)	3·59 g/litre
Ash	2·83 g/litre
Alkalinity of ash	27·9 cc. N/l

Organic acids

Tartaric	1·740 g/litre
Malic	0·590 g/litre
Lactic	1·380 g/litre
Succinic	1·263 g/litre

Mineral anions

Sulphates	0·233 g/litre
Chlorides	0·054 g/litre
Phosphates	0·185 g/litre

An interesting feature is the high amount of glycerine, responsible for a quality often described in Portugal as 'velvety'. It

109

is illuminating to compare this analysis of a *vinho maduro* with that of a *vinho verde* on page 87. The much higher content of acid, especially malic, in the Green Wine is immediately apparent.

The wines

The red wines are dry, strong, deep in colour and full-bodied, resembling burgundies more than clarets; but, as with Riojas, which they resemble not at all, there is little point in pressing the comparison. They possess a smoothness resulting from the slow fermentation and glycerine content, but incline to earthiness of flavour and develop very little nose unless aged for considerable periods in oak and bottle.

The white wines, again blended by the big firms and much less numerous than the reds, have in the past tended to suffer from being aged overlong and losing their freshness. Methods are, however, changing; and wines such as the young white 'Grão Vasco' are aromatic, clean and fruity.

The expansion of the cooperatives and the standards enforced by the Federação have resulted in a general scaling up of quality; some of the red *reservas* are very nice wines, round and well-balanced, and the region now produces a great deal of pleasant and very reasonably priced wine for everyday drinking. The very success of recent measures has, however, militated against the emergence of the individual and exceptional growths of which one feels the Dão to be capable. This is really a matter of history and economics. In the established wine-growing areas of France, Germany and the Rioja, traditions of sophisticated wine-making go back at least a century or more, and private concerns grew up with the resources and expertise to make fine wines from selected varieties of grape. In the Dão, the situation is that all the large firms are tied to buying the bulk of their wine from the same ten cooperatives, so that such differences as emerge are largely the result of greater or less skill in blending and maturing it.

The outcome was well described in a report by *Decanter*'s tasting panel on twenty-five red Dãos from different firms and of vintages ranging from 1975 to 1968:

After tasting the twenty-five wines before them, the panel concluded that Dão reds are very good value for money. There was only a marginal difference between all the wines in quality and taste. David Wolfe summed up the mood of the panel when he said: 'It is by far and away the most consistent group of wines we have tasted. There was no wine which you could not drink with some pleasure. If you bought a bottle of Dão and liked it, then it would be safe to buy almost any other label and get the same satisfaction.'

In Portugal itself, the firms which buy the wine often feel that the cooperatives might go further in meeting their requirements by more careful selection of the grapes—or even by vinifying different varieties separately. Again, since the bulk of the wine is sold in the domestic market, where the taste is for red wines resembling those made in the old *lagares*, there is a tendency to leave the skins (and even stalks) in contact with the must for too long. Excess of tannin can make the young wines hard and bitter in finish; some age and soften very well in oak, while others dry out before losing their astringency. (The fact that the barrels used for ageing the wine are often as large as 3000, 5000 or 7000 litres, with a surface area in relation to volume much lower than that of a 225-litre Bordeaux-style cask, means that maturation must be prolonged to achieve much effect.) It would seem that one solution to the problem is to make a less tannic type of wine for export—something that the cooperatives are reluctant to do!

As regards the white wines, the cooperatives sometimes ferment them at temperatures leading to loss of fragrance and fruit and also tend to play safe by overdosing them with sulphur dioxide—one sometimes suspects that this too has become an acquired taste in Portugal!

I find it difficult to supply a cut-and-dried vintage guide. At tastings organized by *Decanter* and *Caterer and Hotelkeeper* no significant pattern emerged. D. José Rodrigues Sampaio, the very experienced manager of the Vinícola do Vale do Dão, commented that 1954 and 1957 were outstanding and that the last really good year was 1970. Certainly his 'Grão Vasco' 1970 was a beautiful wine, dark orange in colour, with a fruity nose, blackberry flavour, smooth and very dry with a fairly astringent finish. D. Luís Machado of Carvalho, Ribeiro & Ferreira, who make the excellent wines on behalf of the Conde de Santar, agreed that 1970 was outstanding; and in his opinion 1973 was a good year, the 1976 wines lacked acidity and those of 1978, though small in quantity, were excellent.

The favourites of *Caterer and Hotelkeeper*'s panel were a 1969 from Caves Primavera and a 1970 *reserva* from Barrocão, while *Decanter*'s panel chose, by a narrow margin, the 1971 Ribalonga, the Imperial Garrafeira 1971, the 'Alexandro Magno' 1974 and the 1969 *reserva* from Caves Aliança. I might add that one of the Dãos which I have myself most liked in recent years was a 1964 *tinto* bottled by the Federação, on which my notes were: 'dark ruby with orange rim, delicate ethereal nose, extremely dry and smooth, pleasantly acid aftertaste, light for a Dão and a most superior wine'. In general, this assortment of opinions tends to confirm my own feeling that the red Dãos with most appeal abroad are those which have spent a considerable period in wood, so softening the initial astringency and, with adequate age in bottle, heightening the nose and flavour.

The younger 1975 wines are a mixed bag. This was the year following the Revolution, and, as Snhr. Sampaio explained, there was great difficulty in dealing with the cooperatives, since the managers were arbitrarily removed or given menial jobs, and doorkeepers and others who knew nothing about making wine, took over for a period. There *are* acceptable 1975 Dãos to be had, but the wines are less consistent than those of other years.

The Portuguese taste for white Dão is for the older wines, aged in wood, golden yellow in colour and somewhat maderized. Snhr. Sampaio, for example, considered the 1972 one of his best wines. Since 1977, the Vinícola do Vale do Dão has been shipping a younger type of white 'Grão Vasco', pale yellow in colour, flowery and aromatic, and fresh and attractive in taste. Other firms have taken note of the growing foreign demand for young, fruity wine, and are following suit, and another attractive wine of this type is the white 'Meia Encosta' from Borges & Irmão.

Leading suppliers of Dão, culled from the last list of prize-winners in the Concurso Nacional de Vinos Engarrafados organized by the Junta Nacional do Vinho are:

Vinícola do Vale do Dão	'Grão Vasco'
José Maria da Fonseca	'Terras Altas'
União das Adegas Cooperativas do Dão	Dão Adegas Cooperativas

Real Companhía Vinícola do Norte de Portugal	'Cabido'
Caves Fundação	Dão Fundação
Caves Império	'Painel'
Caves São João	'Porto dos Cavaleiros'
Caves Borlida	'S. Vicente'
Caves Aliança	Dão Aliança
Caves Dom Teodósio	'Cardeal'
Caves Velhas	Dão Caves Velhas
Carvalho, Ribeiro & Ferreira	'Conde de Santar'
Caves da Silva	'Dalva'
Ferreira Malaquias	Dão Ferreira Malaquias
Caves Acácio	'Novo Mundo'
Caves Primavera	Dão Primavera
Caves do Solar de S. Domingos	Dão S. Domingos
J. Serra & Sons	Dão Serra
Sociedade Com. Abel Pereira da Fonseca	'Viriatus'

Production of Dão wine in 1980 amounted to 361,367 hecto-litres and exports of bottled wine to 1,465,098 litres of red and 376,848 litres of white. The largest foreign customer was Canada (with 356,013 litres in 1979), followed by Brazil, the United States, Britain (with 136,963 litres in 1979) and Belgium. Large amounts are also shipped to the former Portuguese colonies.

7

Bairrada

The Bairrada, situated in the Beira Litoral, a province flanking the Atlantic and extending from just south of Oporto to the neighbourhood of Coimbra, was only recently demarcated, in 1979. It is a low-lying area, in which small fields of wheat and maize are interspersed with fruit trees, olives and vines, and is not much visited by tourists. Hidden in the forest of Buçaco on its eastern fringe, the Palace Hotel (p. 119) is nevertheless one of the best in Portugal; there is a pleasant waterside *pousada* (a government-run inn, along the lines of a Spanish *parador*) on the great lagoon of Aveiro to the north; and it is with relief that one turns off the overcrowded and dangerous main road from Lisbon to Oporto for such havens of peace as the Estalagem de Pateira, with its excellent Bairrada cuisine and long views over a lagoon, curiously Chinese in appearance, as the occasional flat-bottomed skiff drifts by fishing for the local eel.

The demarcation of the Bairrada has been a heated issue since as long ago as 1908, when plans were drawn up for the other regions, and has been achieved only by constant pressure on the part of the growers.

The region has as long a history of viticulture as any in Portugal, and the Monastery of Lorvão was famous for its vineyards and its wines in the tenth century. In 1137 King Afonso Henriques, the architect of Portuguese independence, authorized the plantation of a vineyard at Vilarinho do Bairro on condition that he should benefit by a quarter of its production, and by the beginning of the sixteenth century its strong red wines were being shipped from the port of Figueira da Foz. There was a major set-back when, concomitant to setting up the monopolistic Oporto Wine Company in 1756, the Marquês de Pombal imposed severe restrictions on the making of wine in the Bairrada, even going so far as to order the uprooting of most of the vines. The restrictions were not lifted until Pombal's dismissal during the reign of Queen Maria I (1777–99); and having weathered the twin disasters of oidium and phylloxera in the latter decades of the nineteenth century, the Bairrada has long since emerged as one of the country's most important wine-growing areas.

Soil and viticulture

The demarcated region embraces parts of the districts of Aveiro and Coimbra, the best of the wines coming from the communes of Anadia, Mealhada, Cantanhede and Oliveira do Bairro. Some 18,600 hectares are actually under vines, farmed by about 7000 growers, the bulk of them smallholders, and producing an annual

Vineyards near Anadia. (Jan Read)

average of 480,000 hectolitres of red wine and 22,000 hectolitres of white (mostly used for making sparkling wine by the champagne method).

The soils consist mainly of clay and limestone; in fact, the very name of the district has been derived from '*bairro*', or popularly '*barro*', meaning 'clay'—though an alternative derivation is from the Arabic '*barri*', signifying a deserted rural settlement. The climate is temperate and less wet than that of the Minho to the north, with an average rainfall of between 900 and 1000 millimetres.

The vineyards, many of them small, are dispersed among the fields of maize and other crops, and the vines are pruned low, growing free or supported by wooden stakes. The predominant black variety, accounting for some 90 per cent of the plantations, is the Baga, the balance consisting of João de Santarém, Castelão, Tinta Pinheira and Bastardo. The main white grape, grown to the extent of some 80 per cent, is the Maria Gomes. Other native varieties are the Bical, Rabo de Ovelha, Arinto and Cerceal; and there are also small plantations of foreign varieties, such as the Pinot Noir, Pinot Blanc, Gamay and Chardonnay, long ago introduced from France and used for making sparkling wine.

Towards the end of the last century, a research station, the Estação Vitivinícola da Beira Litoral, was founded in Anadia to improve techniques and advise the growers. Its first director, D. José Maria Tavares da Silva, did valuable work in selecting suitable phylloxera-resistant stocks and grape varieties; and it was also he who introduced the manufacture of sparkling wine by the Champagne method to the Bairrada, now a most important facet of its wine industry. In collaboration with the Junta Nacional do Vinho, it is now the regulatory body for the region, laying down standards for the production of the wine and issuing *selos de origem*.

It has also played a large part in the planning and operation of the six cooperatives in the region, at Águeda, Vilarinho do Bairro, Mogofores, Mealhada, Cantanhede and Souselas. The largest of these, at Cantanhede, numbers upwards of 900 *associados* and makes an annual average of some 45,000 hectolitres of wine.

The wines

As long ago as 1875 a contemporary oenologist, António Augusto de Aguiar, commented that the red wines were a match for three men—one to drink, and the other two to support him or lay him on the floor. Writing in 1979, D. Octávio Pato of the Estação Vitivinícola agrees that, when young, the wines are hard and harsh in the mouth, but instances this as proof of their breeding, since they soften and improve when aged for as long as twenty to thirty years—or 'as long as the corks will last'.

The reason for this excessive astringency is that the Baga grape, making up 90 per cent of the *encépagement*, is very rich in tannins; and the problem, of course, arises that a commercial winery cannot afford, as a matter of routine, to age the bulk of its wine in wood for prolonged periods. In the past the *marc* was left in contact with the fermenting must for periods of seven to ten days; and if smoother, less aggressive wines are to be produced, the solution would seem to be along the lines of separating the *marc* at an earlier stage. Another recommendation of the Estação Vitivinícola is that the percentage of the Baga be reduced and that some 30 per cent of other noble grapes, such as the Trincadeira, Bastardo and Moreto be substituted. Snhr. Pato is insistent that enough tannin is left in the wine to allow for the traditional maturation in wood and doubts whether the region will ever produce light wines low in alcohol—in any case, it is always a mistake to tamper too much with regional wines of character—and given the splendid quality of the fruit, the red Bairrada should do well in foreign markets.

The traditional white Bairrada was a fairly robust wine with a hint of lemon in the flavour, but very little is now being made, and as Snhr. Pato remarks: 'to talk of white Bairrada is to talk of its sparkling wines'. These are described in Chapter 12, as is the other main product of the region, its excellent *bagaceira* or *marc*.

Leading producers

There are twenty-nine major *caves* in the Bairrada, most of them situated within a 10-kilometre radius of Anadia at the centre of the wine-producing region. They are named as such, rather than *adegas*, because much of their output is of sparkling wine (see

Chapter 12). Many, like Aliança, Barrocão, Borlido, Império, S. Domingos and S. João, mature and market Dão under brand labels; Messias bottles a good *vinho verde*; and almost all produce very drinkable *aguardente* (or brandy) made in pot stills, as is their *bagaceira* (or *marc*).

The largest of the firms is Caves Aliança, situated in Sangalhos, a busy little wine-making town a few kilometres to the west of the main Lisbon–Oporto road. It ranks next in size to SOGRAPE and J. M. da Fonseca, but in terms of domestic sales is second only to SOGRAPE; and its reliable 'Tinto Velha Aliança', made mainly from Bairrada wine, is the biggest-selling red wine in Portugal. Aliança was founded in 1920 and is still controlled by the Neves family. It owns few vineyards of its own, so that most of the grapes are bought from independent farmers. Both the red and white wines are aged in oak, either from Limousin or from the neighbouring forest of Buçaco.

Some of the best red Bairrada is made by the smaller concern of Caves São João, whose energetic and infectiously enthusiastic proprietor, D. Luís Costa, has not only amassed fascinating records of wine production in the area, but also played a leading part in forming the Confraría dos Enofílos da Bairrada, a fraternity devoted to enhancing the quality of the wines and to making them more generally known.

Perhaps the most reliable guide to current vintages of Bairrada is that of the Portuguese expert Dr. Lopo Cancella de Abreu, who lists what he considers to be the eleven leading *caves* (with the date of foundation in brackets) together with their best wines.

Monte Crasto (1890)   White, seco; red, Tinto Velho.
Solar de Francesas (1905)   White, seco; red, Garrafeira 1963 and 1968.
São João (1920)   White, 1976; red, Reserva Particular 1970, Reserva Frei João 1970, Frei João 1975.
Barrocão (1920)   White, Garrafeira 1968 and 1970; red, Garrafeira 1970 and 1974.
Borlido (1920)   White, Garrafeira 1971; red, Garrafeira 1966 and 1971.
Aliança (1920)   White, Garrafeira 1970; red, Garrafeira 1970.
Messias (1928)   White, Garrafeira 1960 and 1970; red, Garrafeira 1970, 1973 and 1976.

Neto Costa (1930)   Reputed for its sparkling wine, brandy
   and *bagaceira*.
S. Domingos (1936)   White, Reserva 1977; red, Reserva 1970
   and 1974.
Montanha (1940)   Red, 1967.
Império (1942)   White, Garrafeira 1966; red, Garrafeira 1966
   and 1970

It is most instructive to taste the red Bairrada, *mano a mano*, as
the Spaniards say, with a red Dão of the same age. The Bairradas
retain their plummy colour much longer, are more tannic and
require longer in oak to soften. They are predominantly wines
which repay prolonged ageing in oak and bottle. A favourite red
Bairrada of my own is, for example, the 1960 Garrafeira
Particular from Barrocão (sold at an extraordinarily modest price
considering its age). My impressions were: 'Deep ruby colour.
Delicately fruity nose with touch of cedar wood, opening up as the
wine stays in the glass to become fruitier and sweeter. Soft fruity
flavour with a hint of cedar wood, but still tannic at the end. A
very pleasant wine.'

Buçaco and its wines

Beyond Mealhada on the main road and tucked away to the
extreme east of the region in the forests of the Buçaco mountains—
the 'damned long hill' where Wellington defeated Marshal
Masséna in 1810—is a majestic hotel which offers a splendid local
wine. The 'green cathedral' of the forest, with its steeply winding
roads and great flight of stone steps, is worth the visit in itself. It
includes 400 different varieties of tree, native and foreign: ginkos,
monkey-puzzles, sequoias, palms, thuyas and Himalayan pines,
interspersed with hydrangeas, tree ferns, magnolias, camellias
and sheets of lilies of the valley, to mention only a few.
   The hotel, set in a forest glade amongst decorative gardens, was
planned as a grandiose summer pavilion and hunting lodge by the
King-Consort Dom Ferdinand. It was built for him in neo-
Manueline style by the Italian architect Luigi Manini and
decorated with splendid *azulejos* representing the Battle of
Buçaco, but was only briefly used by the royal family, since King
Carlos I was assassinated a year before its completion in 1909 and

119

his successor, Manuel II, was deposed in 1910, when Portugal became a republic.

It owes its splendid cellar to a gifted hotelier, Alejandro de Almeida, who took over the palace in 1916 and began making the now famous Buçaco wines, maturing and bottling them at the hotel itself. Production is small, amounting to an average of 25,000 to 30,000 litres of white and 30,000 to 40,000 litres of red, all of it still made by treading the grapes in stone *lagares* in traditional fashion. Outside Buçaco the wines are obtainable only at the other hotels under the management of the Almeida family: Das Termas at nearby Curia, the Astória at Coimbra, the Metrópole in Lisbon and the Praia-Mar in Carcavelos.

The reserves in the cellars at Buçaco amount to some 200,000 bottles, and the knowledgeable manager of the hotel, D. José Santos rates the vintages as follows:

White Buçaco

1944	*****	1965	*****
1950	***	1966	*****
1951	***	1967	***
1952	**	1968	***
1953	****	1970	****
1955	***	1972	****
1956	*****	1974	***
1958	**	1975	****
1959	***	1977	***

Red Buçaco

1927	*****	1961	***
1940	*****	1962	***
1945	***	1963	*****
1949	***	1964	**
1951	****	1967	****
1953	*****	1970	****
1955	***	1972	****
1957	****	1974	***
1958	*****	1975	***
1959	***	1977	***
1960	****		

My own favourites are the reds, which are almost claret-like in

The cellars of the Palace Hotel at Buçaco, whose fine reserves amount to
some 200,000 bottles. (Jan Read)

their fruitiness and intensity of flavour. My notes on the exceptional 1953, which had been aged for three years in wood and thereafter in bottle, and threw a heavy deposit, were: 'Deep orange colour. Intense fruit in the nose and flavour. Soft and velvety with a long finish. Magnificent.' On an earlier visit, I noted of the 1959: 'Bright, tawny-coloured, with a light fruity nose. Well-balanced, a little astringent, but not unpleasantly so. Good finish. A most elegant wine.'

Hugh Johnson, who recently stayed at the hotel and was able to taste a much wider range of vintages, has most kindly sent me his notes.

Of the reds, he writes:

My favourites were the '60, like a powerful claret in beautiful young condition, and the heavenly '53. We had two bottles of the '27—both tawny, but lovely and elegant with the delicious hint of resin that seems to be endemic.

The *rosado* is excellent, somehow crisp, but full of flavour. It was the '77. The only wine we did not like at all was the 'Meio Doce' medium sweet '63—thin and tired; but the brandy (really *marc*) is fine.

His detailed notes on the whites, made with 45 per cent Bical, smaller amounts of Maria Gomes and Malvasia, and a trace of Moscatel, are as follows:

1977   Adequate, rather light; the main effect rather resiny wood.
1968   Delicate and very pleasing, but again rather light and too woody for me.
1966   Very pale. Rich, almost *moelleux* flavour with a hint of the aromatic honeyed style of Condrieu. Excellently balanced, with the oak under control.
1965   Pale amber. Extremely good, round and full, but with almost as much oak as e.g. 'Tondonia' [a white Rioja from López de Heredia].
1956   Remarkable. More complete than the '65 with a little more richness.
1944   The oldest listed. Mid-amber, fine and almost dry. Frail now, and hinting at caramel. On its way out, but still charming.

Undemarcated Wines of the North

Apart from the extensive vineyards of the Ribatejo, Torres Vedras and Cartaxo, just north of Lisbon, which in the main produce *consumo* wine for everyday drinking (see Chapter 10), there are a number of regions in northern Portugal whose wines are none the less attractive for being undemarcated.

UPPER DOURO

As already mentioned (p. 34), the largest of these regions, the Upper Douro, is now on the way to demarcation; various localities have been recognized as 'determinate areas' by the EEC Commission, and their table wines rank as 'Quality Wines PSR'. Though it is not officially classified, pride of place among its growths must go to the famous 'Barca Velha', which is, in fact, among the very best of Portuguese table wines, made in very limited amount and enjoying the same prestige as the legendary 'Vega Sicilia' in Spain.

'Barca Velha'

The problem in making a good Douro table wine has always been to control the speed and temperature of fermentation, and 'Barca Velha' (the name refers to the old sail boats used for ferrying wine down the Douro) was evolved after the chief taster for the Port firm of Ferreira, D. Fernando Moreira Paes Nicolau de Almeida, had made lengthy investigations in Bordeaux, consulting, among others, the renowned Professor Peynaud. This was many years ago, and Snhr. Almeida, accustomed to the open granite *lagares* of the Douro, told me of the surprise with which he then viewed the Bordeaux-style vats, asking how the treaders could work in such confined spaces!

The wine is made at Meão, in a wide loop of the river at the top of the Douro valley, only 40 kilometres as the crow flies from the Spanish border. The Quinta do Vale de Meão was one of the numerous properties belonging to Dona Antónia Adelaide Ferreira, the uncrowned Queen of the Douro and largest landowner in the region—when she died in 1896, Meão alone was valued at £3 million. The great house was one of the many between which Dona Antónia divided her year; the portrait of her friend the Baron Forrester still hangs in the dining room, and her spirit broods

Vineyards and olive groves bordering the River Douro near the Quinta do Vale de Meão, where the famous red 'Barca Velha' is made. (Jan Read)

heavily over the empty reception rooms and echoing corridors, furnished as they were when she was last in residence.

When I was last there, her great grandson, Jorge Ferreira, improved the occasion by telling us how, late in life, the elderly Duque de Saldanha, then the strong man of Portugal, wished to enliven his blue blood with that of the Ferreiras and proposed marriage to her only daughter. Dona Antónia would have none of it and barricaded herself and Maria da Assunção in another of her *quintas* at Travassos near Régua, whence they escaped, disguised as peasants, first to Vigo and then to London, where they sojourned for three years awaiting the Duke's death.

Long, low and stone-built among the olive groves near the river, the *adega* where 'Barca Velha' is now made was one of Dona Antónia's most ambitious projects. Originally built in 1892 for making Port, it was a marvel of Victorian technology: a grand staircase leads up to the fermentation hall, some 100 metres long, with its serried rows of granite *lagares* for the treading of the grapes, each requiring a gang of forty men (Ferreira still uses the traditional method for its select Ports). Underneath the *lagares* were stoves to initiate fermentation in cold weather, and they were further provided with an ingenious system of pipework to blend grape spirit into the raw wine as it poured into casks on a lower floor.

The *adega* is still mainly used for Port, but it also houses vats for making the 'Barca Velha'. These were formerly of oak, but the new stainless steel tanks now being installed should make it easier to control the temperature of fermentation and to increase production—in the past vintages have been somewhat irregular. Before adopting the new system, Ferreira are, however, making wine side by side in oak and stainless steel to compare the quality.

The wine, all of it red, is made from a blend of three Port grapes, Tinta Roriz (60 per cent), Amarela (15 per cent) and Touriga Francesa (20 per cent) with the addition of lighter, more acidic grapes grown in the same schistous soil, but on high ground some 30 kilometres down the valley to the south and bought from independent farmers. After spending a year or so in oak, the wine is matured for a much longer period in bottle at Ferreira's lodge in Vila Nova de Gaia.

Two vintages are available at the time of writing, the 1965 and 1966, both in minuscule supply and obtainable only in Portugal

125

itself at the best restaurants and hotels. Both are a deep ruby-orange with an intensely fruity nose and flavour, round, full-bodied, complex and beautifully balanced. Of the two, the '66 has the slight edge in depth and length. To give some further idea of their quality, I would say that the wines which they most resemble are 'Vega Sicilia' (from the same valley, but in Spain, where the river is known as the Duero) or the beautiful Australian 'Grange Hermitage'. Although Ferreira made a wine with somewhat similar characteristics in 1974 and 1977, sold as 'Ferreirinha Reserva Especial', they did not consider that any of the vintages of subsequent years until those of 1978, 1979 and 1980 were of sufficient quality to bottle as 'Barca Velha'. It is early days to judge the 1980, which is as yet a deep blackberry colour with a yeasty nose, masses of fruit and extract, and a dry, tannic finish.

Other wines from Trás-os-Montes

The main wine-producing area of this large and mountainous province, lying to the north of the Douro, is the Vila Real region including the districts of Chaves, Valpaços and Vila Pouca de Aguiar; but wines, mainly red and rosé, are made as far afield as Bragança in the extreme north-west near the Spanish border. Besides Vila Real itself, Sabrosa and Alijo, where there is a *pousada* named in honour of the Baron Forrester (see p. 41), have recently been named 'determinate areas'. Average annual production runs to 215,000 hectolitres of red wine and rosé and 20,000 hectolitres of white.

The soils of this high plateau are mainly pre-Cambrian schists with outcrops of naked granite, and many of the vineyards are planted on hillsides flanking the minor tributaries of the Douro to the south. The predominant grape varieties are the black Bastardo, Tinta Amarela, Tinta Carvalha, Moreto, Tourigo and Alvarelhão, and the white Boal, Códega, Gouveio and Tarrantez.

The wines vary a great deal over the region, resembling neither those of the Douro valley proper with their high sugar content, nor those of the Vinho Verde region to the west with their *pétillance* and low degree of alcohol. For example, the red wines of Valpaços near Chaves are dark, full-bodied and high in alcohol, while those of Boticas and Carrazedo, further north and higher in altitude, are more like the Minho wines. Those most generally available (apart, of course, from the branded rosés described in Chapter 11) are the Vila Real *claretes* from SOGRAPE, made at the same winery as 'Mateus Rosé' in Vila Real itself, and 'Evel' from the Real Companhía Vinícola do Norte de Portugal, both to be found on most Portuguese wine lists.

A good place to taste a wider range of regional wines is the Palace Hotel at Vidago, 40 kilometres north of Vila Real and near Chaves. This is an old-fashioned and splendid Edwardian spa hotel, at whose past glories one can only guess, set in beautiful wooded grounds embracing an elegant pump room, its own post office (now abandoned) and a bandstand among the trees. The lofty, wooden-floored dining room with its musicians' gallery offers a lengthy wine list, with bottles at modest prices that have been slumbering in the cellar for years. Among those which I tried on a recent visit was a non-vintage 'Evel' (at least some ten years old), orange-ruby in colour, with pronounced 'legs' in the glass, a raspberry nose, fruity flavour, soft and long on the finish. Highly recommended by the head-waiter was an old cooperative-made Valpaços. Though a mature and fruity wine, full-bodied, orange-ruby in colour and with a raspberry nose and flavour, I found this distinctly acid.

LAFÕES

Lafões is a small region, with an annual production of 80,000 hectolitres of red wine and 8000 hectolitres of white, wedged between the demarcated areas of the Vinhos Verdes and Dão, and has recently been designated a 'determinate area'. It embraces the district councils of São Pedro do Sul, Vouzela and Oliveira de Frades; the parishes of Lordosa, Bodiosa, Calde, Campo and Ribafeita (belonging to Viseu); and also the parishes of Alva, Gafanhão, Cedrim and Couto Esteves.

Part of the upper basin of the Mondego River, it is a very hilly area, hemmed in by mountains. The soils are characterized by granite and schists, and the climate is Atlantic and very wet, with a rainfall often in excess of 2000 millimetres. The red wines are made from Castelão, Moreto, Martágua, Rufete and Trincadeira grapes, and the whites from the Arinto, Alva, Cercial, Polgazão and Tamarez.

127

Though somewhat akin to the *vinhos verdes* in their fragrance and high acidity, the typical red wines are fuller-bodied and improve with maturing.

BEIRAS

The centre of this mountainous region between the Dão and the Spanish border is the old fortress town of Guarda—the highest in Portugal at 1040 metres. The most productive wine-growing area of the district is the lower Côa, north of Guarda in the Beira Alta. Pinhel, in this northern area, has long been known for its white wines, somewhat similar to those of the adjacent Dão, and Meda, still further north and not far south of the Douro, is now a 'determinate area'.

As in this part of Portugal generally, the soils are again largely granitic and schistous. The red wines are made from the black Marufo, Rufete, Bastardo and Mourisco grapes, and the white from the Codo, Fontegal, Arinto, Malvasia and Alva. One white wine deserving special mention is the Malvasia from Moimenta da Beira, light, acidic and low in alcohol, and particularly suitable for making *espumantes* or sparkling wines by the Champagne process (see p. 152).

As a whole, the Beira Alta produces some 150,000 hectolitres of red wine and 36,000 of white in an average year. The Beira Baixa, south of Guarda, is less important as a wine-making area, but produces both red and white wines from around Covilhã and Belmonte. Covilhã, in the wooded foothills of the Serra da Estrela, has stronger claims to gastronomic fame in the form of its ewe's milk cheese, the excellent Queijo da Serra (see p. 169).

The Quinta da Insua in the Dão, a headquarters of Wellington during the Peninsular War. Its tiny adega makes a Cabernet Sauvignon wine. (Jan Read)

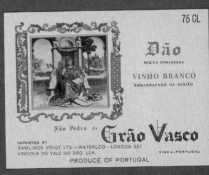

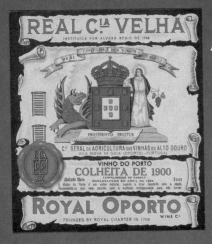

Portuguese wine labels.

9

The Wines of the South

For reasons both of history and climate, Portugal south of the Tagus produces far less wine than the northerly regions.

Since the time of the Moors, its empty sun-baked expanses have been the province of large landowners, more interested in using the land for pasturage, for growing cork oaks, or for the cultivation of olives and cereals rather than of the vine.

As in the south of Spain, the long, hot summers also pose problems in the making of quality wines, since the grapes are so rich in sugar that, when fermented by traditional methods, they yield wines overstrong in alcohol, inky black in colour and 'chewy' in taste because of their superabundance of extract. Here, at least, matters are changing with the introduction of closed vats, first developed in Algeria to cope with similar problems, and modern methods for the control of temperature during fermentation.

Only two of the regions south of Lisbon have been demarcated, those of Moscatel de Setúbal (at present being redefined—see p. 72) and Algarve; but in view of the increasing importance of their wines, Palmela in the Arrábida Peninsula just south of Lisbon, and Borba, Reguengos and Vidigueira in the far east of the Alentejo towards the Spanish border, have been designated 'determinate areas'.

THE ARRÁBIDA

There has already been mention of the Arrábida Peninsula (pp. 71–5) in connection with Moscatel de Setúbal, but when José Maria da Fonseca founded his firm in Azeitão in 1834, he by no means confined himself to perfecting the famous dessert wine.

The grape with which he made his first wines was the local Periquita, which in fact takes its name from the small farm, 'La Periquita' (Portuguese for a 'small parrot'), where he started operations.

The Periquita is now widely grown in the Alentejo, but the best-known of the wines to be made from it remains the original 'Periquita' from Fonseca. Although in his *Portuguese Wine* Raymond Postgate dismissed it as 'a red ordinaire ... in no way exceptional', H. Warner Allen ranked it with Colares as 'a wine very attractive for the combination of great silkiness of texture such as graces a fine Burgundy with stout body and a sweet flowerlike scent.' Like all of the red wines from J. M. da Fonseca, it is aged in wood, and I have always found it sound, pleasant drinking and excellent value at its very modest price. It also keeps well once the bottle has been opened and is as good on the second day as the first.

My notes on a range of red wines made by Fonseca at their Old Winery in Azeitão were as follows:

> '*Periquita*' *1975.* Made entirely from Periquita grapes, more than half the wine is grown and vinified by Fonseca, the rest being bought from local growers. Dark ruby, raspberry nose, very dry, a little acid and somewhat lacking in character.
>
> '*Periquita*' *1977.* A better wine with less astringency.
>
> '*Pasmodos*' *1971.* Made from a blend of Alentejo grapes. Dark ruby, scented nose, softer with a raspberry taste. Pleasant.
>
> '*Camarate*' *1974.* This wine was formerly sold as 'Palmela', but now that Palmela has been designated a 'determinate area', only wines made from grapes grown in the immediate environs may be labelled as such. The *encépagement* for 'Camarate' is a blend of Cabernet-Sauvignon, Periquita and Merlot grapes, and the presence of Cabernet is evident both in the nose and the light, somewhat claret-like flavour. An attractive wine, with its fruity finish.
>
> '*Garrafeira P.*' *1974* (two years in wood). Ruby colour. Nose a bit faint when cold, but improved in a warmed glass. More of the velvety taste of a good Dão.
>
> '*Garrafeira*' *1964* (a blend of Alentejo wines with three to four years in wood). Dark ruby colour. Deep oaky nose. Full-bodied, but drying out.

The Old Winery of J. M. da Fonseca at Azeitão. (Jan Read)

Fonseca's huge New Winery at Azeitão, used mainly for making sparkling rosés (see Chapter 11), also incorporates cellars with a capacity of 2 million bottles for maturing the wines made at the Old Winery down the road. An interesting departure has been the setting aside of a small area for 225-litre chestnut casks, used for the maturing of a straight Cabernet Sauvignon wine made from grapes grown on the 2 hectares of the near-by Quinta de Bacalhoa. It is yet too early to judge the success of this experiment—but the Quinta itself, Moorish-inspired and set in formal gardens with a pool and pavilions decorated with *azulejos*, is quite enchanting.

A pleasant place to try the local wines is at the government-run *pousada*, installed in the magnificent Castle of Palmela, with its wide views across the Arrábida and the Bay of Setúbal. But perhaps the most atmospheric venue for a bottle of 'Periquita' or 'Camarate' is the delightful Quinta das Torres,[1] an *estalagem* (or inn) directly opposite the New Winery and hidden from the road at the top of a long tree-lined lane.

With towers at the corners and a wide courtyard planted with orange trees at the centre, it resembles a small Italian palace and, in particular, the architectural phantasies of Rafael. The dining room, overlooking a pool overhung by great trees, is embellished with two splendid majolica panels representing the burning of Troy and the construction of Carthage, of Italian origin and dating from about 1570; and the food, simple but sophisticated, is worthy of the elegant surroundings. A favourite dish with visitors from Lisbon is the *bacalhau dourada*, creamy and golden yellow, and one of the most delicious versions of the dried and salted cod so popular in Portugal (see Chapter 14).

ALENTEJO

The immense province of the Alentejo, stretching from the Atlantic to the Spanish border for much of its length, occupies almost a third of the total land area of Portugal. Its wide plains are seen to their best in the late spring and early summer, when one

---

[1] There are details of the fascinating history of the Quinta das Torres and the Quinta de Bacalhoa, both at one time in possession of the same family, in J. M. Dos Santos Simöes, *Panneux de Majolique au Portugal*, in *Faenza, Bolletino del Museo Internazionale della Ceramiche in Faenza*, 1964, Fascicolo III–VI.

drives along roads flanked by dazzling yellow broom, through expanses of fresh green corn and rolling pasturage carpeted with wild flowers, variegated by shimmering grey-green olive groves and sallow scrubland dotted with the darker cork oaks.

A good centre for visits to its vineyards is Évora, a walled town since Roman times, but predominantly Moorish in character, with brilliant white houses, tiled patios, narrow arched alleys and hanging gardens. Among its main sights are the pillared Roman temple, the granite-built Gothic cathedral and the Largo dos Portas de Moura, with its twin towers, part of the medieval fortifications commanding the northern entrance to the town, and the beautiful Renaissance fountain at its centre.

The Pousada Dos Lois, built in 1491 as a monastery dedicated to St. Eligius (or Eloi), is a most attractive place to stay. Beautifully furnished in period, it has kept its Manueline arches, marble staircases and silent cloisters; and its cool bedrooms are installed in former monastic cells. There are also a number of good restaurants hidden in the side streets, at one of which I was once fortunate enough to track down a few bottles of the elusive 'Barca Velha' (p. 123).

There are three main wine-growing areas, producing between them an annual average of 76,000 hectolitres of red wine and 50,000 hectolitres of white. Beja and Vidigueira (a 'determinate area') south of Évora make mainly white wine; Reguengos de Monsaraz and the 'determinate areas' of Redondo and Borba, to the west near the Spanish border, are best-known for their full-bodied reds; while Portalegre, further to the north, makes both red and white wines.

The soils derive from the Palaeozoic or Primary period, and the climate is dry; the region suffers from prolonged droughts, and the annual rainfall seldom exceeds 60 millimetres. The predominent varieties of black grape are the Trincadeira, Periquita, Tinta Caiada, Monvedro, Castelão and Moreto; while the white wines are made mainly from the Boal, Arinto, Pendura, Assario, Rabo de Ovelha, Roupeiro and Tamarez.

In general, the red wines are to be preferred to the rather 'earthy' whites, which sometimes suffer from being vinified at temperatures up to 35°C. In the past, black and white grapes were often fermented together in large earthenware containers, *tarefas de barro*, resembling the *tinajas* of Montilla or Valdepeñas in

133

Spain. These are still occasionally to be found in the private *adegas*, but the bulk of the wine is now vinified in the cement vats or more modern steel tanks of the cooperatives. (The Alentejo was, of course, one of the regions which most strongly supported the 1974 revolution and the expropriation of absentee and private landowners; and on the walls of the cooperatives one often sees slogans demanding that the wine be marketed direct and not sold to private firms for their branded marks.)

The wines which are making the most impact outside the region are the reds from the eastern area, the bulk of it produced by the cooperatives of Reguengos, Redondo and Borba. A typical *encépagement* for the reds is:

40% Periquita
30% Moreto
15% Trincadeira

A typical white wine might contain:

50% Formosa Dourada
30% Manteudo
15% Roupeiro Cachado

In both cases, the balance is made up with smaller amounts of other varieties.

The cooperatives keep their wines, both red and white, in cement *depósitos* before bottling them and do not possess wooden casks for maturing the *reservas*, which are simply kept in the *depósitos* for a further few years. To my mind, this does not improve them, but leads to their becoming somewhat resinous in nose and stale in flavour.

The best of the reds are the *vinhos do ano* ('wines of the year'), and there is little to choose between those from the three cooperatives. Of the young wines which I have tasted, the best is the well-made young Borba, a dark damson in colour, with a yeasty, fruity nose, a deep blackberry flavour, mouth-filling because of the high amount of extract and with a good fruity finish. It would be most interesting to see how such an attractive young wine would develop if properly matured in cask. My note on a typical *reserva* (from Reguengos) runs: 'Still a dark plummy colour, not much fruit in the nose, slightly resinous, peppery nose and flavour, not altogether pleasant. Much prefer the younger.'

The cooperative at Reguengos de Monsaraz in the Alentejo. (Jan Read)

Concrete 'balloons' for the bulk storage of wine at the Cooperativa de Reguengos. (Jan Read)

The best of the white wines are also the youngest. As already mentioned, they sometimes suffer from being vinified at temperatures in excess of 30°C, but the best of them (from Redondo), pale straw-coloured, is fresh in nose and flavour, though 'earthy' in finish. The *reservas* lose their freshness and emerge a deeper yellow, sometimes with a lemon flavour.

All of these wines are high in alcohol, the whites approaching 12·5°, and the reds 13·5°, so that a half-bottle between two people is often enough—though with a hearty dish of the local *sopa alentejana*, a thick potage containing *bacalhau* (dried and salted cod), poached eggs, bread, potatoes and red peppers, a bottle goes down easily enough!

There is also a well-reputed private *adega* in Reguengos, that of J. S. Rosado Fernandes, making superior red Alentejo wine from

The cellars of J. S. Rosado Fernandes in Reguengos, makers of a superior red Alentejo wine. (Jan Read)

grapes grown in its own vineyards near the town and planted in the proportion of 60 per cent Periquita, 30 per cent Trincadeira and 2 per cent Bastardo.

This is one of the establishments which still ferment the wine in earthenware *tarefas*, subsequently maturing them in its beautifully kept and spotlessly clean sanded cellars containing barrels ranging in size from 6000 litres downwards, and giving them further age in bottle. My notes on the wines were:

Tinto do ano Deep, plummy colour. Young, yeasty nose. Fruity flavour. Sound.

Tinto 3° ano Dark ruby orange. Blackberry nose and flavour. Dry. Nice.

Tinto 4° ano Still quite a plummy red. Very dry and astringent at the end.

Tinto 1971 Damson colour. Delicate fruity nose with a little oak. Fruity, fresh and well-balanced.

Rosado Fernandes also makes a brandy in the traditional pot stills. After five years in wood, it emerges a brilliant amber colour, mellow and fragrant on the nose. A small amount of the red table wine, presented in bottles with *arame* (fine wire mesh, like that used in the Rioja), is shipped to the UK.

ALGARVE

The wines from the Algarve do not strictly belong among the undemarcated wines discussed in this chapter, since the region has recently been demarcated, but they seem apiece with others from the south. They are better known to foreign visitors than many of the others from Portugal because of the thriving tourist industry; and though the agriculture of the region is primarily devoted to almonds, dessert grapes and market gardening, there is a long tradition of wine-making. It is known traditionally for a dry white apéritif wine, matured in wood and of some 15° strength, made from the Crato branco grape, whose musts grow a *flor* (or film of yeasts) like those in Jerez.

The wine-growing area is a narrow strip lying between the Atlantic coast and the Monchique and Caldeirão mountains to the north. Of the average annual production of 70,000 hectolitres, all but 3 per cent is red, made from the Negra Mole, Trincadeira, Periquita, Monsedro, Crato Preto, Bastardo, Pau Ferro, Pexém and Moreto grapes. The white varieties are the Crato branco, Boais, Manteudo, Tamarez, Sabro and Perrum.

Although acceptable enough holiday drinking on a terrace with a view of sparkling sands and blue water, the wines, most of them made in cooperatives at Lagoa and Portimão, are not particularly distinguished, the reds tending towards low acidity and containing upwards of 13° of alcohol.

10

Wines in Bulk

What the wines of La Mancha and Valdepeñas are to Spain, those of Torres Vedras and its associated districts, and of the Ribatejo, are to Portugal. Especially in parts of the Ribatejo, the vines grow in low unbroken expanses reaching as far as the eye can see, with production approaching a million litres per square kilometre; and these large regions rather north of Lisbon are the main suppliers of *consumo* wine to the capital.

OESTE

In terms of bulk, the so-called 'Oeste' or Western Region, extending northwards from the Tagus estuary to Óbidos and Caldas da Rainha, and from the Atlantic to the Ribatejo in the east, is the most important in the country. It falls into two sub-zones, that of Torres Vedras, Alenquer and Arruda dos Vinhos in the south, and of Alcobaça in the north.

Torres Vedras

The hilly country around Torres Vedras forms a natural barrier, famous because Wellington made use of it during the Peninsular War to construct a continuous line of fortifications, some 50 kilometres long from the Atlantic to the Tagus, so as to halt the advance on Lisbon of the French army under Marshal Masséna. As Masséna's aide-de-camp relates,

Instead of the 'undulating accessible plateau' that we had been told to expect, we saw steeply scarped mountains and deep

139

ravines, a road passage only a few paces broad, and on each side walls of rock crowned with everything that could be accomplished in the way of field fortifications garnished with artillery.

So successful was Wellington's manoeuvre, that after sitting out the winter of 1810–11, the French army retreated in disarray, a repulse from which it was never to recover.

Above the town of Torres Vedras, and only about a kilometre and a half from the modern cooperative, the fortifications remain much as they were in Wellington's time—stone walls, a great stone-faced fosse, watch towers, magazines and a small chapel—perched above the undulating, sunlit vineyards.

The soils in this area consist mainly of calcareous clay, and the climate is mild with an average annual rainfall of 600 to 700 millimetres. The red wines are made from Periquita, João de Santarém, Tinta Miuda and Castelino grapes, and the whites from the Vital and Bual.

The cooperative at Torres Vedras is one of the largest in Portugal; its grapes are supplied by 1800 *associados* owning on average some 5 hectares of vineyard, and the storage capacity runs to 16,500,000 litres. The wine is vinified in concrete vats with provision for automatic submersion of the 'cap' (*autovinificadores*) and also, in the case of the inexpensive red wine, by a continuous process in large steel tanks. Some 60 per cent of it is sold in bulk, the rest being bottled at the cooperative. As well as red, white and rosé wines, the cooperative makes a *bagaceira* (see p. 157) and a *licoroso*, a fortified wine in the style of a rough tawny Port—but drinkable nonetheless.

Of the white wines, I preferred the *vinho do ano* ('wine of the year'), straw-yellow in colour, dry and refreshing, if lacking pronounced character. A 1972 white, aged first in *depósito* and then in bottle, was lemon-yellow in colour, with somewhat oily nose and flavour, reminding one of bitter almonds. Both were completely dry and of about 11·5° strength.

The red wines contain upwards of 12° of alcohol. The young *vinho do ano* which I tasted at the cooperative was a deep cherry-red, full-bodied with a fair degree of fruit in the nose and flavour, and very dry. The older reds are not aged in wood, but spend several years in bottle—five years in the case of the 1970, which struck me as oily and flat both in nose and taste. I preferred the

1971, a dark damson colour, with more fruit in the nose and a blackberry flavour, also rounder and better-balanced, but still very dry in finish.

Alenquer and Arruda dos Vinhos

Over towards Alenquer and Arruda dos Vinhos on flatter land nearer the Tagus, there is another large cooperative at Dois Portos; and the white wine of Alenquer was shipped to England as long ago as the fourteenth century. One of the most interesting private *adegas* in the area is the Quinta de Porto Franco, owned by the Correia family (one of whose sons is manager of the Torres Vedras cooperative, and another its oenologist).

Lying among cherry orchards and set in a decorative garden, the winery is a rambling old building housing concrete vats and barrels of Hungarian oak in a variety of sizes for ageing the wines. Its 400 hectares of pine-fringed vineyards are planted with the black Periquita, Tinta Muera and Camarate grapes, and the white Vital and Jampal. Production is very sizeable, and the wine which is not aged at the *adega* is sold off to large firms for blending and marketing under brand names. Its own red wines, with their blackberry flavour, high degree of extract and dry finish are typical of the area, but sometimes suffer from being bottled before secondary fermentation is complete, so displaying a slight *pétillance*.

Alcobaça

Traditions of wine-making in this undulating region further to the north go back to the twelfth century, when viticulture was introduced by the monks of the historic monastery of Alcobaça, famous as the resting place of Inês de Castro. The typical white grapes are the Rabo de Ovelha, Vital, Fernão Pires, Boal de Alicante and Malvasia, while the reds are made from the João de Santarém, Baga and Castelão.

One of the pleasantest wines from the area is the red Gaeiras from Óbidos, a small hilltop town some 10 kilometres inland from the Atlantic and one of the most picturesque in Portugal, with its balconied houses gay with flowers, its medieval walls and narrow streets, crowned by an old castle, now converted into a *pousada*.

Of the wine, Steven J. Schneider has recently written in his *International Album of Wine*

'that this agreeable, light, and nicely scented red has such a reputation is perhaps due to the dense, astringent, overpowering qualities of most other Portuguese wines, compared to which the softness of Gaeiras is notable. Foreigners will enjoy rather than revere this wine, which is produced in small quantity. Lately a local white wine, produced from the Vital variety, has won greater fame and is now the most sought-after white in Lisbon.'

RIBATEJO

Santarém, on the west bank of the Tagus overlooking the vast plain of the Ribatejo, of which it is the chief town, is a place rich in historical associations. Perhaps the most romantic episode in its long history was its recapture from the Moors in 1147, when Afonso Henriques, lacking the siege engines to take it by frontal assault, overcame its defenders at dead of night by stratagem. In granting a Royal Charter to the town in 1170, Afonso required 'the villagers to surrender one eighth of the bread, wine and flax produced in the region'. There were many subsequent royal decrees during the medieval period—so, on 18 February 1364, Dom Pedro I forbade the entry into Santarém of wines from outside the area until the Day of Santa Maria in August 'because of the enormous expenses disbursed in fertilizing the vineyards', while in the reign of Afonso V (1438–81) 'foreigners were exempt from paying taxes when carrying and transporting wine by boat from the neighbourhood and confines of the borough of Santarém to the outside world . . .'

The wine-growing region, mainly north of the Tagus, includes the districts of Azambujo, Cartaxo, Rio Maior, Santarém, Almeirim, Alpiarça, Chamusca and Salvaterra de Magos. In terms of output, the region ranks second only to that of the 'Oeste', producing in an average year some 63,000 hectolitres of red wine and 750,000 hectolitres of white.

The soils are mostly sedimentary and, besides alluvium, contain clay, clay-limestone and some sand. The climate is sub-

Mediterranean and mild, with an average annual rainfall of 500 to 600 millimetres. The best of the red wine, full-bodied, dry, dark in colour and high in alcohol and extract, are made around Cartaxo, a little to the south of Santarém, from the Trincadeira, Mortágua and João de Santarém grapes. The white wines, again high in alcohol, are sound and fruity, but incline to heaviness and 'earthiness'. The main white grapes are the Fernão Pires, Terrantez, Rabo de Ovelha, Boais and Jampal.

There are a number of large cooperatives in the region—at Cartaxo, Gouxa, Almeirim and elsewhere—but one of the best-known wineries is that of Carvalho, Ribeiro and Ferreira at Vila Franca de Xira, on the bank of the Tagus where the first of the bridges north of Lisbon crosses the river.

Carvalho, Ribeiro and Ferreira was founded in 1898 and is sixth in size of the larger Portuguese wine firms. It does not vinify any wine, but buys it already made, blending and ageing it in the extensive cellars at Vila Franca. Apart from marketing the local Ribatejo wines under its label, the firm is the largest brandy-maker in the country (see p.154); it also sells a good 'Ravel' *vinho verde* made at Farmalicão and handles the excellent Dão from the Conde de Santar (see p. 107), maturing and blending it at Vila Franca (under the supervision, of course, of the Federação dos Vinicultores do Dão). Another interesting product is an old *vinho licoroso* from the Estremadura, a maderized white wine of quality, somewhat sweet with a dry finish and rather resembling a Verdelho Madeira.

Some of the old Ribatejo *garrafeiras* from Carvalho, Ribeiro and Ferreira are very fine, and I have a note in particular on the Garrafeira Cosecha 1961, an old blended wine, still a deep ruby in colour, smooth and elegant with a blackcurrant nose and flavour.

The wines for which the firm is best known are, however, the red and white 'Serradayres'. By these there hangs a tale. 'Serradayres' ('Mountain of Air') was originally made near Borba (see p. 134), in the Alentejo beyond Évora. Carvalho, Ribeiro and Ferreira bought the name and now make it by blending wines from the Ribatejo to correspond as closely as possible to the original. For all this, the red 'Serradayres', the more characterful of the two, is a great deal lighter than any red which I have tasted in the Alentejo and more like a *clarete* in style. It is matured in large wooden *toneis* (barrels) ranging in capacity from 30,000 litres to 7200 litres and

Bottles of 'Serradayres' maturing in the cellars of Carvalho, Ribeiro and Ferreira at Vila Franca de Xira in the Ribatejo. (Jan Read)

5420 litres. Smooth, fruity and well-balanced, the red 'Serradayres' in various vintages appears among the *vinhos maduros* on most Portuguese wine lists, and is a pleasant alternative when one tires a little of the body and astringency of some of the other wines.

144

11

Rosé Wines

Portugal's sparkling rosés are the commercial success story of the present century, as was Port before them in the eighteenth and nineteenth centuries. In 1980 foreign shipments ran to some 41 million litres, accounting for 65 per cent of all exports of bottled wine and representing a major contribution to the country's economy.

Connoisseurs do not often display the same enthusiasm for even the best of rosés, like Tavel, as for a vintage red or white wine. In the nature of things they tend to be a compromise, refreshing in hot weather, but short-lived and lacking strong individuality. Nevertheless, the Portuguese rosés with their crisp bubble and fruity flavour have won an army of friends all over the world. Especially in the United States they have introduced a vast new public to wine-drinking; their manufacture has involved a technical revolution; and their marketing and distribution clearly foreshadow the shape of things to come.

As far as Britain is concerned, the story begins when Sacheverell Sitwell 'discovered' 'Mateus Rosé' in 1951, writing in his weekly column in the *Sunday Times* that it was 'the most delicious vin rosé that I have ever tasted . . . Mateus is delicious beyond words; and since I am told that it will travel and is exported to Brazil, it is a pity that one cannot buy it here in England.' Events have since moved full circle. In1980 the United Kingdom imported 343,320 cases, accounting for 11 per cent of the world market; 'Mateus' is now the first choice of the businessman or hostess who feels that it will 'go with anything'—meat, fish or sweet—while writers on Portuguese wines perversely give it only a few perfunctory sentences, which is clearly absurd.

There are numerous other firms, like Aliança, C. da Silva,

Borges & Irmão and the Real Companhía Vinícola, which make and market sweet carbonated rosé wine, but the giants in the field are SOGRAPE, who produce 'Mateus', and José Maria da Fonseca, makers of 'Lancers' and 'Faisca'. There has been frequent mention of these companies before, and both are, of course concerned with a great deal more than rosé, including Dão, *vinhos verdes* and regional wines.

D. Fernando van-Zeller Guedes, whose energy and capacity for organization are behind the success story of 'Mateus Rosé', might fairly be described as the doyen of the Portuguese wine industry and beyond that an unofficial ambassador for his country. Among his ancestors are a sixteenth-century viceroy of Portuguese India, a van Zeller (a famous name, of course, in the history of port) who in the fourteenth century was a Marshal at the court of the Duke of Gueldres in Holland, and Thomas Maynard, appointed first British consul in Oporto by Oliver Cromwell. A courteous and accessible man with a keen sense of humour, he has never allowed the huge size of SOGRAPE to prevent it from being run as a family firm, and the personal interest of the Guedes family in the well-being of their employees bore fruit at the time of the Revolution in 1974. I was told by D. José Rodrigues Sampaio, manager of the Vinícola do Vale do Dão, how there was a movement in Oporto to nationalize SOGRAPE. Workers from the outlying establishments organized buses to go to the crucial meeting, and when the vote was taken hardly a hand was raised in favour of a take-over.

The Guedes family is linked by marriage with the other great wine dynasty and their business competitors, J. M. da Fonseca. After the death in 1884 of the original José Maria da Fonseca famous for his Moscatel de Setúbal (see p. 72), control of Fonseca passed through marriage and inheritance to Dr. Antonio Soares Franco, whose sons began production of 'Lancers' for the US market immediately after the Second World War.

Viticulture and grape varieties

Production of the sparkling rosé wines was first begun at Vila Real, north of the demarcated Port region in the province of Trás-os-Montes, and was later extended to the Beira Alta, the Bairrada and the Setúbal Peninsula. The Ministerial Order of 11 August

1979 has defined in detail the areas within the regions most suitable for growing grapes for the rosé wines. These include: in Trás-os-Montes, various communes around Vila Real and Guarda; in Beira Alta, a large number of parishes around Viseu; in the Beira Litoral, a variety of districts around Anadia, Mealhada and Coimbra; and Palmela and Sesimbra, near Setúbal. To meet the growing demand, the production of grapes is also authorized in Torres Vedras and other areas north of Lisbon; in the Cartaxo near Santarém; near Évora in the Alentejo; and around Faro in the Algarve.

As regards grapes, the Order lays down that at least 60 per cent of the plantations must be of one or more of the following approved varieties:

Trás-os-Montes Tourigos, Tinta Amarela, Tinta Francisca, Tinto Cão, Mourisco and Alvarelhão.

Beiras Rufete, Marufo, Tourigas, Tinta Amarela, Tinta Carvalha, Baga and Alverelhão.

West Ribatejo João Santarém (Santarém, Trincadeira or Periquita), Tinta Miuda, Camarate (Mortágua), Castelão and Preto Martinho.

Algarve Negra Mole, Trincadeira (Periquita), Monvedro, Bastardo, Pau Ferro, Pexem and Moreto.

The Order further requires that the maximum production of wine is not more than 60 hectolitres per hectare.

Vinification

The plants employed by the large firms for the vinification, elaboration and bottling of the rosé wines are among the largest and most sophisticated in the world.

The wines are usually made by the process of *bica aberta*. This involves the destalking and crushing of the grapes; the skins are then allowed to stand in contact with the must for a short period to withdraw colouring matter; and fermentation then proceeds as for a white wine, without the presence of skins and pips. The residual sweetness may be achieved either, as with 'Mateus Rosé', by centrifugation of the must or the addition of sulphur dioxide so as to remove the yeasts from the sphere of action before fermentation is complete, or by the addition of *mosto amuado*. This is a partially fermented or concentrated must; and the Ministerial Order provides that it may not be added in quantities which would increase the alcohol content by more than 2° (or 2 per cent by volume).

Vinification and bottling are normally carried out at separate establishments. SOGRAPE operates two vinification centres, one at Vila Real with a production capacity of 9 million litres, used exclusively for the vinification of Douro wines, and another at Anadia in the Bairrada, capable of handling 14,000 tonnes of grapes, with additional capacity planned for a further 14,000 tonnes. With its batteries of centrifuges, its great refrigerated stores and endless stainless steel tubing, this must be one of the

Centrifuges for clarifying wine at the great modern winery of SOGRAPE at Anadia. (Jan Read)

148

most advanced wine-making plants in existence. A new departure is that the familiar concrete 'balloons' (see p. 106) are used not only for the storage of wine in bulk, but also for fermentation of the must.

Further treatment and bottling

Once the wine has been vinified it is taken by road tanker to plants which are even more impressive in scale—surrounded by tank farms of gleaming white concrete 'balloons' for the preliminary storage of the wine, these establishments are straight from the space age. The main buildings house lines of tiled or stainless steel vats in diminishing perspective, miles of stainless steel connective tubing, and elaborate pumping, filtration and refrigeration machinery, often operating without sign of human agency. Where the humans come into their own is in the huge bottling areas, where the automated lines are staffed by scores of spotlessly uniformed girls, whose cheerful chatter is drowned by the clatter of the myriad bottles as they jostle along the conveyor belts.

SOGRAPE's central bottling plant, with a storage capacity of 20 million litres of wine, is located among gardens and pine trees at Avintes outside Oporto; and although operations may appear dehumanized, the firm takes a lively interest in the welfare of its 600 workers at the store and has built a community centre, complete with canteens, nursery school, surgery and recreational facilities.

Fonseca's spacious New Winery at Azeitão is hardly less impressive. Beneath a new extension to the building are arched cellars with kitchens and an entertainment area seating 2000 people, used for large tastings and for entertaining the employees on festive occasions. A separate workshop in the grounds makes the traditional terracotta-coloured ceramic flasks used for 'Lancers'—though the wine sent to the USA (some 1,500,000 bottles annually) is now bottled in similarly shaped glass jars, spray-painted on the outside in the bottling plant.

The methods used by SOGRAPE and Fonseca are very similar. From the 'balloons', the wine passes to huge stainless steel or cement *depósitos*. It is then filtered through kieselguhr and blended in even larger *depósitos*. After blending, the wine is refrigerated in great tanks to precipitate solid matter and is then filtered twice through kieselguhr before a final filtration through a cellulose membrane to remove the finest particles. Filtration through asbestos has been abandoned on health grounds.

The sparkle is not natural, but is achieved by passing a small amount of carbon dioxide gas from cylinders into the refrigerated wine at a pressure of five atmospheres.

The SOGRAPE operation is entirely Portuguese; Fonseca, while retaining 51 per cent financial control, planned and built their new plant at Azeitão in partnership with Heublein Inc., their American importers and distributors of, among other things, Smirnoff vodka. Both firms send the lion's share of their exports to the USA—amounting to 37·1 per cent in the case of SOGRAPE in 1980. In order of importance the other leading foreign markets for 'Mateus' are the UK, Canada, Italy, Germany, Japan, the Netherlands, Australia, Sweden and Denmark.

A great deal of care is devoted to the design of bottles and labels, undertaken with the advice of the foreign distributors. Perhaps most familiar is the distinctive 'Mateus' flagon, shaped like an Armagnac bottle, with its attractive picture on the label of the beautiful Mateus Palace, adjoining the winery at Vila Real. By this hangs a tale—no doubt apocryphal. The aristocratic owner, so the story goes, was offered a royalty on each bottle of 'Mateus'. He opted instead for a lump sum amounting, as it subsequently turned out, to only one year's royalty on current sales.

The wines

These wines are so well-known in Britain and America as to need little description here. The style varies from firm to firm and is largely dictated by the distributor and based on extensive market research. It is, however, worth pointing out that a wine such as 'Lancers' is not a standard product, but is elaborated differently according to the market for which it is destined. During a recent visit to Azeitão, I made the following notes on the Fonseca rosés:

Faisca Rosé. Very pale pink. Fresh rosé nose and taste. Fruity and fairly dry. Contains less sugar than most. Agreeable.

Lancers Rosé. Darker colour. Fruity nose. Fresh, slightly sweet, but with a dryish aftertaste. Pleasant.

Lancers Rosé (American-style). This is the 'Lancers' as I remember it, sweet and much aerated.

Both the Ministry of Agriculture and the producers are making efforts to upgrade the rosés, both by stricter definition of grape varieties and the areas in which they may be grown, and by making wines for the European market that are less sweet and carbonated. As regards the USA, it is a question of going along with the distributor and providing what the customer demands.

Apart from the wines from SOGRAPE and Fonseca, others to have won medals in the Concurso Nacional in recent years are:

'Casal Mendes' and 'Aliança seco'	Caves Aliança
'Casalinho'	Caves do Casalinho
'Lagosta'	Real Companhía Vinícola do Norte de Portugal
'Isabel'	C. da Silva
'Infants Vintage seco'	Caves S. João
'Trovador'	Borges & Irmão
'Impérial'	Caves Império
'Casaleiro'	Caves Dom Teodósio
'Messias seco'	Companhía dos Vinhos Messias
'Grandelite'	Ca. Geral Agricola Vinhos Alto Douro

Sparkling and Aromatic Wines: Spirits

Sparkling wines

Sparkling wines have been made in Portugal on a fairly large scale since the last quarter of the nineteenth century, though not much is exported, except to Brazil. They are made both by the traditional Champagne process and also in *cuves closes*. As in Spain, they may not be sold as 'Champagne', but are known as *espumantes*.

In outline, the *espumantes naturais* (those made by the Champagne method) are prepared from wine vinified by *bica aberta* or *en blanc*, after the removal of stalks, skins and pips. A little sugar and cultured yeasts are added, and the bottles are then closed with temporary corks or crown caps and binned away in cool underground cellars until such time as the added sugar has been broken down into alcohol and carbon dioxide. After a period of years, the bottles are placed in the familiar wedge-shaped wooden frames or *pupitres*, the angle of which is gradually altered, so that, starting in a slightly inclined position, the bottle ends up almost on its head with the sediment in the neck next to the cork. During this period the bottles are given a slight angular twist each day to promote the descent of the sediment—a process charmingly described by a brochure from Caves do Barrocão, in a brave translation of the French *remuage*, as 'daily mooing in the proper phase'! Although some of the *cavas* employ a mechanical device for altering the angle of the bottle and giving it the periodic angular twist, the *girasols* (metal frames) now much used for this purpose in Spain have not been introduced to Portugal.

The final stage is to freeze the neck of the bottle and to remove the temporary stopper, when the pressure of gas inside the bottle expels the sediment in the small block of ice at the top. *Liqueur d'expédition* is added to top up the contents, and, depending on its sugar content, the *espumante* may be *bruto* (extra-dry), *seco* (fairly dry), *meio seco* (in practice, a bit sweet) or *doce* (sweet). Pink *espumantes* are made by allowing limited contact with the skins during the original fermentation, and I have even drunk a deep red *tinto* from Caves Barrocão in the Bairrada—though this, I feel, is an acquired taste!

The less expensive *cuve close* wine is made, as elsewhere, by conducting the secondary fermentation, not in individual bottles, but in closed tanks, and bottling it under pressure. It is, of course, still much preferable to sparkling wines of the 'Champagne type' made by pumping carbon dioxide under pressure into still wine.

In the main production area, the Bairrada, north-west of Coimbra (see pp. 114–19), the predominant grape used for its sparkling wines is the white Maria Gomes, but *espumantes* are also made in Lamego and Oporto; and other grapes which have been found to be very suitable are the Arinto, Rabo de Ovelha, Bical and Pinot. These are not always grown locally, the other main suppliers being the Dão region, Moimento da Beira, Tarouca and Pinhel.

Practically all the firms already mentioned in connection with the Bairrada—Aliança, S. João, Messias, Império and the others, as well as Borges & Irmão and the Real Companhía Vinícola in Oporto—make good-quality sparkling wines by the Champagne process, though in comparison with Champagne from Reims or the crisp *espumosos* from the Penedès in Spain, they tend, although very fruity, to be somewhat heavy and 'earthy' in finish.

My own favourite, which I find rather lighter than some of the others, is the *bruto* from Caves da Raposeira in Lamego, a small hill town rather south of Régua and the Port region. It is a most picturesque little place, noted for its really excellent ham cured in the style of the Spanish *jamón serrano* (p. 170), rich in sixteenth-, seventeenth- and eighteenth-century houses, and dominated by the great baroque sanctuary of Our Lady the Redeemer, set among hanging gardens and approached by flights of granite steps, springing, as it seems, direct from the centre of the town.

Raposeira is an old-established family concern, and although it

153

has recently been taken over by the Canadian firm of Seagram, I am assured that it is only the labelling and not the character of the wines which has changed.

The cool and extensive *caves* are tunnelled into a hillside above Lamego, and when I last visited them some years ago the wine was still being made in barrels, and I was received by the Valle brothers in a small office lined with large sepia photographs of their ancestors and loud with the rumble of casks from the unseen depths below. They are among the most genial and hospitable *vignerons* in Portugal with an infectious enthusiasm for their wine; and it is pleasant to record that António Valle still acts as consultant to the new management.

To avoid partiality, it seems appropriate to end with a list of the *espumantes naturais* to win gold medals at the last Concurso Nacional:

Avo—*meio seco* and Super Messias—*bruto*	Sociedade Agrícola dos Vinhos Messias
Bruto—Raposeira	Caves da Raposeira
Dalva—Grande Reserva—*meio seco*	C. da Silva (Vinhos) SARL
São Domingos—*bruto*	Caves Solar de S. Domingos
Sautomar—*bruto*	Real Cave do Cedro

Vermouth

Though Italy and France have a virtual monopoly of the international market for vermouth and aromatic wines, Portugal, like Spain, does make some of the well-known brands under licence. For example, Cinzano and Martini are made by Portuguese offshoots of the firms that originated them; and Dubonnet is manufactured under licence by J. M. da Fonseca, which also produces 'Cherrybom', a liqueur, as they describe it, embodying 'the perfume of the blossom, and the taste of the fruit of Portugal's cherry trees'.

Brandy

Brandy is called *aguardente* or *aguardente de vinho* in Portugal to distinguish it from the popular *aguardente de bagaceira* or *marc*, commonly referred to simply as *bagaceira*.

Continuous column for making grape spirit from vinho verde *at the distillery in Palmeira, near Braga, operated by the Comissão de Viticultura da Região dos Vinhos Verdes. (Jan Read)*

As in Spain, the cheaper brandies are made from a grape spirit containing some 77 per cent by volume of alcohol, distilled from surplus wine in a tall, steam-heated column by the continuous process. This is supplied to private firms by the government-controlled Administración Geral de Alcool (see p. 84) and is subsequently diluted with water to a strength of about 44° and matured in oak casks. Inexpensive brandies of this type, though often light in colour, are on the sweet side and somewhat manipulated and flavoured, with a pronounced taste of vanilla.

However, most of the larger wine firms make a better quality of brandy on the premises by the traditional Charentais process, using small pot stills. (The position is very different from that obtaining in Spain, where government regulations forbid the manufacture of brandy and table wines in the same bodega.)

This method allows for much greater control over the final product, the first and third fractions of the first distillate, the 'headings' and 'tailings', being rejected, while the middle fraction, the 'heart' or *brouilli*, is returned to the still for further distillation. The raw brandy is run into oak casks to mature, and the strength is later adjusted to about 40° by addition of water. A little sugar is added and a modicum of caramel to deepen the colour. Although brandy-makers do not publicize it, there may also be further small additions of natural flavouring matter, such as toasted almond shells or dried prunes.

There is a very wide range of these older and smoother brandies, the best being labelled *reserva, velha, vehissima* or *antiquíssima* ('old' and 'very old'). The areas generally considered to make the wines most suitable for brandy are the Vinho Verde region; Lafões, a small enclave between the Vinho Verde region and Dão; and the Bairrada.

The largest producer is Carvalho, Ribeiro & Ferreira in Vila Franca de Xires, just north of Lisbon, which makes part of its brandy in a small continuous still some 8 metres high. The best of its marks is the thirty-year-old 'Aguardente Preparada Reserva', only slightly caramelized, light in colour with a pungent nose, but smooth aftertaste. Other brandies which I have myself enjoyed are: 'Velha' and 'Antiquíssima' from Aliança; 'Velha' and 'Antiquíssima' from Barrocão; Delaforce 'Fine Brandy', Ferreira 'Reserva' and Kopke, from the Port firms of the same names; Messias; and 'Espirito' from J. M. da Fonseca.

Perhaps most like a French cognac, or even more like an Armagnac in its lightness and delicacy, is the 'Adega Velha' from the Sociedade Agrícola da Quinta de Aveleda. It was evolved with advice from D. Amândio Barbedo Galhano, formerly of the Comissão da Região dos Vinhos Verdes and also responsible for the beautiful Alvarinho from the Palacio de Brejoeira. Double distilled by the Charentais method from red *vinho verde*, it is aged in oak and only very lightly caramelized. The French brandy-makers have been so impressed by its quality as to look into the possibilities of themselves using musts from grapes grown in the Vinho Verde area for distillation.

In conclusion, I feel that a description of the old brandies from Caves do Barrocão (from the pamphlet already mentioned) is too poignant to be lost—the spelling is all their own:

Born at BAIRRADA, the famous wine District of Portugal, from golden grapes and destille by the old CHARANTEE METHOD, after a long and quiet sleep I became very old.

From the oak barrels where it slept for so many years I took the Yellow ambar coulour breathing through the wooden pores. I lost my roughnesse and god the sweet velvet taste due to a selecte old brandy. My linage and the time I have lived made me what I am. Remember always my name

BARROCÃO OLD BRANDY

Bagaceira

Aguardente de bagaceira or *bagaceira* is a water-white spirit distilled from *bagaço*, the grape skins and pips left over from the fermentation of wine, in the manner of the French *marc* or Spanish *orujo*. It is even more popular in Portugal than brandy and is made all over the country, almost every rural cooperative possessing its own small distillery on the premises. Some of the best and freshest-tasting is made in the Bairrada, where it is the custom to distil the *bagaço* while still moist from the wine presses.

On occasion it is a spirit of some violence to be sipped minimally and with care (CAUTION! some of the rougher varieties may contain methyl alcohol). According to Raymond Postgate, 'it is best in my opinion not to drink *bagaceira* (or any other *marc*) at all'. This, to my mind, is to do it an injustice. Some of the *bagaceiras*, especially those from the Minho, like the popular 'Verdegar' or the more expensive 'Cepa Velha' from Vinhos de Monção, are fruity in nose and smooth in flavour. A good tip is to serve them in a brandy glass with a lump of ice, when (inured to the taste, as I am) I have found them delicious as a *digestif* after dinner.

For people who wish to experiment, those to win gold medals at the last Concurso Nacional were:

Pot still for making bagaceira *at the installations of the Comissão de Viticultura da Região dos Vinho Verdes at Maia, outside Oporto.*
(Jan Read)

A.B.	Caves São João
Casal de Vale Pradinhos	Maria Pinto de Azevado
Fundação—Bagaceira do Minho	Caves Fundação
Irmãos Unidos	Caves São João
Morgarinha—Bagaceira do Minho	Joaquim Miranda Campelo & Filhos
Mosca	José Maria da Fonseca, Sucrs.
Ponte de Barca	Adega Cooperativa de Ponte da Barca
Rumor—Bagaceira do Minho	Caves Dom Teodósio
São Domingos	Caves de São Domingos

13

A Note on Cork

Corks are an essential element in the maturing and the preservation of fine wines, and it seems appropriate that Portugal, which herself produces so much good wine, should be the largest producer of cork and cork products, accounting for 52 per cent of world supplies. In Britain, for example, 96 per cent of cork stoppers are imported from Portugal, 2 per cent from Spain and the remaining 2 per cent from five other countries.

Corks have been used for stoppering wine for thousands of years. They were employed for this purpose by the Assyrians, Egyptians, Greeks and Romans, but then fell out of fashion until the end of the seventeenth century, when they were reintroduced and Dom Pérignon (possibly obtaining them from Catalonia) used them for stoppering Champagne, so retaining its natural sparkle. Their use in combination with a cylindrical bottle, which made possible the prolonged maturation of wine in glass (see p. 24) originated in Oporto about 1770.

The value of cork in this connection is that it is a vegetable material, free from toxic ingredients, and does not impart odour or taste. It is also impermeable and forms a tight seal, both because it is elastic and expands against the inside neck of the bottle and because the cells at the surface are ruptured during manufacture, forming minute cups, which produce a vacuum as the cork is forced into the neck and so ensuring a high degree of adhesion to the glass.

Good corks retain their impermeability for very long periods. In 1939 a number of wine jars, dating from the third century and stoppered with cork, were discovered in France, and the contents were still drinkable. That one occasionally comes across a bottle of 'corked' wine does not always result from a defective cork—

though there are, of course, corks that become so porous and soft that they disintegrate in the process of removing them. More frequently the 'woody' or musty taste of a 'corked' wine is caused by lack of hygiene during its making or bottling.

Apart from preserving the wine, the impermeability of the cork also plays a most important role during its maturation, which takes place in two stages. After secondary fermentation is complete and the wine is racked and transferred to wooden casks, it undergoes a limited and very slow process of oxidation brought about by the transpiration of air through the pores of the wood. This is necessary for the development of a good red wine (but not necessarily for a white). Thereafter, in bottle, both types of wine, again extremely slowly, undergo a complex series of chemical reactions, including the reverse process of chemical reduction, thought by some authorities to contribute to the fragrant bouquet. During this stage in the wine's development (and, of course, until the bottle is finally opened) it is essential that contact with the atmosphere should be minimal. No better way of ensuring this has been devised than a sound and tightly inserted cork, with its myriads of self-contained cells (40 million per cubic centimetre). Each is sealed off from the next by five separate membranes: two cellulosic and elastic, two containing the waxy water-impervious suberin, and the other lignified and more rigid.

Cork is made from the bark of the cork oak (*Quercus suber*), a native of the Western Mediterranean area; and production of the raw material is limited (in order of their importance as producers) to Portugal, Spain, Algeria, Morocco, France, Italy and Tunisia. The forests in Portugal extend to some 1 million hectares and are distributed up and down the country, but the dark green cork oaks are most frequently to be seen in the Alentejo and Algarve, where they are a feature of the landscape.

Regulations for the protection of the cork forests date from the fourteenth century. Bark cannot be stripped from the trees until they are twenty to twenty-five years old; and there is a legal requirement that subsequent stripping may not take place at intervals of less than nine years, so as to allow for the physiological recovery of the tree.

The bark is stripped from the trunk of the tree in large slabs during the summer, when growth is at its most active. It is then taken to one of some 600 factories, most of them near Oporto or

Setúbal, for processing. This consists in placing layers of the sheets in a large concrete tank and boiling them under heavy pressure so as to remove certain mineral salts and impregnated tannins and to flatten them, at the same time making the cork softer and more elastic. The sheets are then scraped, dried and selected for different uses. Only the thickest and most finely grained are suitable for the best-quality corks.

Stoppers were formerly made by cutting square sections from the large boards and trimming the edges. Nowadays the boards are cut into strips and the corks are punched out mechanically. Since this leaves them slightly elliptical in section, they must further be trimmed to the exact dimensions. The waste material is ground and used for a variety of purposes, including the cheaper composite stoppers and the liners for crown caps.

The typical cork factory is a busy and animated place, loud with the whirr of the scores of punches and trimming machinery and blanketed in fine dust. In fact, the industry in Portugal employs some 20,000 workers.

The manufacture of stoppers, accounting for 59 per cent of the value of exported cork products, is a trickier and more complicated operation than would seem at first sight, involving as it does a large diversity of types—stoppers and bungs, Champagne, imitation, cylindrical, tapering, whisky, etc., to name only a few. Each of these may be made in a large number of different sizes, with tolerances of only a fraction of a millimetre and dimensions ranging from a diameter of 2 millimetres and a height of 9 millimetres to diameters of 120 millimetres and thicknesses of 50 millimetres. The importance of accurate size and thorough inspection is illustrated by the grisly story told me by the manager of one of the largest firms about the rejection of 5 million stoppers, slightly out of size, by three Portuguese cooperatives.

One of the most complicated types of stopper to produce is the traditional Champagne cork. This is specially made to withstand the pressure of gas within the bottle and to prevent its escape. The bottom part is composed of slices of natural cork cemented together so that the grain runs in different directions; to this is affixed an upper section of a softer granulate, and the lower part of the cork is lightly waxed to facilitate the broaching of the bottles. Before use, the stoppers are not the familiar 'mushroom' shape, but cylinders some 30 millimetres in diameter and 50 millimetres long—one wonders how they are ever inserted into the bottles.

The cork firms are not, of course, solely concerned with the manufacture of stoppers. D. Roberto da Costa of A. Paulo Amorim & Filhos mentioned that one of the specialities of his firm is the large cork inserts for the helmets used by the London police; and as cork is also used in motor cyclists' crash helmets, it seems that the Portuguese cork manufacturers contribute not only to our pleasure in drinking wine but also to our physical safety!

14

Food with Wine
by Maite Manjón

If Portuguese cooking is to be compared with that of any other nation, it must be with Spain's. It is interesting to see how the Portuguese and the Spanish, making use of identical raw materials (varying, of course, from north to south and from the seaboard to the common border), have in some respects gone their own ways and yet produce many dishes that are basically the same: roasts of sucking pig, baby lamb and kid, *gaspacho*, a profusion of grilled and fried fish, splendid *mariscos* (or shellfish), a range of cured hams and *chouriços* (Spanish, *chorizos*) and a variety of Moorish-inspired sweetmeats made from eggs and almonds.

Portuguese food at its most individual and interesting is to be found in the smaller restaurants and at the houses of friends rather than in the large hotels, which provide 'international' cooking (meaning, in effect, steaks, veal escalopes, expensive shellfish, grilled or fried sole etc.) enlivened with the occasional Portuguese standby, such as *caldo verde* (cabbage soup) or the cured *presunto* ham. And in the new luxury hotels it is an even bet that visitors from across the Atlantic, having studied the wine list and earnestly consulted the wine-waiter, will opt for one of the sparkling rosés with which they are familiar at home.

Portugal is small, and with its increasing popularity as a holiday area and the development of fast road transport, the best of the dishes originally confined to individual regions may now be encountered up and down the country. *Caldo verde*, for example, which originated in the Minho, and *bacalhau* (salted and dried cod) are now equally popular in the Algarve to the far south.

The widest range of restaurants is naturally to be found in

164

Lisbon and Oporto, and simply by choosing from the first two or three listed in the red *Michelin* it is easy to select a luxury restaurant, like the Portucale in Oporto with its panoramic views and sophisticated cuisine, or the Avis and Tavares in Lisbon. These are the places to go for a really good steak, for Portuguese shellfish at its superb best and for a long wine list. But do not overlook the Alfama, the old Moorish quarter of Lisbon, among whose maze of steep and narrow streets are to be found numerous tiny places where dishes like the grilled *peixe espada* (scabbard fish) are cooked individually and to perfection. Again, the famous Oporto tripe is usually at its best in unpretentious places such as Abadia.

The food at the government-run *pousadas* is uneven and does not always match up to the beautiful surroundings; at that of Elvas, near the Spanish border on the main Lisbon–Madrid road, it has always been outstanding.

One or two restaurants stand out for first-class food—among my favourites are the sophisticated Quinta das Torres near Setúbal (p. 132) and the Palace Hotel at Buçaco (p. 119), also the Cortijo in Viseu with its wide range of local fare.

There are still things which are best eaten in their place of origin. Naturally the best and freshest fish is to be found along the coast; and in fishing villages like Nazaré and Peniche, sardines, shellfish and *caldeiradas* (fish stews) are prepared in individual style. The richest soups and stews of lamprey hail from the Minho, and the best *cozidos* or meat stews, with which a red *vinho verde* is an excellent accompaniment, are made in the north, as befits the cold and wet winters. A favourite and substantial dish from the Alentejo is the *açorda*, a garlic soup containing eggs, potatoes and slices of bread. Oporto remains justly famous for its inimitable *tripas* (tripe), and Lisbon for its *iscas* or liver. The best sucking pig (*leitão*) is still roasted in the open-air ovens of Mealhada, just north of Coimbra, and the delicious cream cheeses of Azeitão are at their freshest around the village south of Lisbon and the Tagus, from which they take their name.

Nevertheless, to give a balanced idea of the range of Portuguese cookery, it seems most sensible to describe the dishes in the conventional way, progressing through the menu from appetizers and soups to fish, poultry, meat and sweets. When in doubt, the Portuguese usually choose a white *vinho verde* with light food and a red Dão, 'Serradayres' or one of the Upper Douro reds with more substantial fare.

Appetizers

A pleasant custom is for the waiter to put on the table small pots of *manteigas compostas* (savoury butters) while one is waiting for the meal proper. These are made by mixing soft, unsalted butter with savoury flavourings, such as ground anchovy, tuna fish or shredded red peppers; and the danger is to eat too much with the excellent fresh bread before the main dishes arrive. Another attractive starter is the *rissóis* (tiny crisp-fried rissoles) made from flaked *bacalhau* in a béchamel sauce. Especially in hot weather, a cool glass of *vinho verde* with its refreshing *pétillance* is the ideal apéritif, though it is also worth experimenting with dry white Port—drunk chilled and much improved with a slice of lemon.

Soups

The most famous Portuguese soup is *caldo verde*, made from chicken broth and the finely shredded leaves of the dark green *couve* (Portuguese cabbage, often grown beneath the trellised vines in the Minho) and thickened with a little potato. It is traditionally eaten with *pão de broa*, a dark-coloured bread baked with mixed rye and wheat flours and made to perfection at Avintes near Oporto.

Excellent *sopas de marisco* (seafood bisques) are obtainable all along the coast. The Alentejo in the south is the home of a *gaspacho*, resembling the cold, uncooked soups from Andalusia, but differing from them in that the peppers and other vegetables are puréed and that they contain chopped *chouriço* or *presunto* (highly cured sausage or ham). Another speciality of the Alentejo is the *açorda* or *sopa alentejana*, which is a meal in itself, since in addition to the ingredients already described (p. 136) it may also contain chunks of *bacalhau*. It is with this that the dark, full-bodied and 'chewy' red wines of Borba, Reguengos and Redondo come into their own.

Fish

Although the markets of Nazaré, Cascais and the Algarve overflow with a splendid variety of fresh fish, most popular in Portugal itself is *bacalhau*, the dried and salted cod whose history has been described (p. 21). Eaten plain-boiled with potatoes it is dull fare, but the ways of preparing it are legion—it is said that there is one for every day of the year—and range from *bacalhau a la vizcaina*, made Spanish-style with a spicy sauce of onions, tomatoes and peppers, to *bacalhau a transmontana* garnished with belly of pork or bacon, or the creamy *bacalhau a lisbonense*. Like kedgeree in consistency, this is entirely delicious at the Quinta das Torres (where it appears, confusingly, as *bacalhau dourada*—a name used elsewhere to describe yet another and completely different version). The more fully flavoured styles of *bacalhau* will easily stand up to a red wine or may be accompanied by one of the full-bodied, maderized whites, so much liked by the Portuguese.

Among the many other excellent fish dishes, only a few of the most individual can be described. *Caldeirada estilo Nazaré* is a rich fish stew, containing both whitefish and shellfish and somewhat akin to *bouillabaisse*. The fresh sardines grilled over charcoal on the beaches are first-rate, and their oiliness is well-relieved by a red *vinho verde* or an astringent red Bairrada wine. In the Algarve, a variety of fish, including cockles and clams, is cooked in a *cataplana*, a domed metal container in two halves fitting tightly together—a precursor of the modern pressure cooker. And a most imaginative way with clams is *carne de porco a alentejana*, now served the length and breadth of the country, in which the shellfish is cooked with tender cubes of fried pork.

When the quality of fish, like sole, is good, there are many, of course, who will prefer it plain grilled; and the best accompaniment to delicate whitefish is either a white *vinho verde*, one of the younger and fruitier white Dãos or a regional wine like the light and crisp Bucelas.

Poultry and game

Chicken is cooked in a variety of ways and goes very well with *arroz açafrão* (rice cooked with chopped onions and saffron) or *arroz de manteiga* (buttered rice). The regions best known for their game are the Ribatejo, just north of Lisbon, and the Alentejo further south. The Ribatejo is also known for its *pato guisado*, duck stewed with chopped onion and carrot and slices of banana and mandarin. This calls for a nice old *garrafeira* from the Ribatejo or the lighter red 'Serradayres'—always a safe choice if one wants an alternative to Dão. A favourite at Christmas is *peru recheado com castanhas* (turkey stuffed with chestnuts). It was the custom in Portugal to make the turkey tipsy on brandy before killing it. This was done neither for sentimental reasons nor as part of the seasonal celebrations, but with the strictly practical object of making the meat whiter and more tender.

Meat

The best roast meats are kid *(cabrito assado)* and loin of pork *(lombo de porco)*; *bifes* (beefsteaks) are to be avoided in any but expensive restaurants, since they may well come from a cow rather than a heifer. In the form of *leitão assado*, the milk-fed lamb is exceptional, the best coming from the Bairrada, and the best from the Bairrada from the open-air ovens of Pedro dos Leitões in Mealhada—and with this it would be a solecism to drink anything but a really nice red Bairrada *reserva* or *garrafeira* or one of the glorious old Buçaco wines.

The Minho in the far north is celebrated for its rib-warming stews or *cozidos*, sometimes cooked with the addition of chick peas and also known as *ranchos*. From the north, too, hail the *tripas a moda do Porto* (tripe), famous since the fifteenth century, when the people of Oporto built the ships for Prince Henry the Navigator's voyages of discovery, victualling them, as the story goes, with the prime meat from their herds and leaving themselves with little to eat except the tripe. The tripe from Oporto differs from the *dobrada* further south and is made with dry haricot beans, *presunto* and *chouriço*, and spiced with curry powder.

Port is, incidentally, rarely used by the Portuguese for cooking, and although the Instituto do Vinho do Porto has produced an interesting booklet of recipes utilizing the wine, they are of recent origin.

Sweets

Although many of their wines are dry and astringent to a degree, the Portuguese have a very sweet tooth—as is evident from the half-dozen packets of sugar served with coffee at breakfast!

As in Spain, the most popular sweet is the ubiquitous *pudim flan* (baked caramel custard), but there is a variety of others, including the delicious *tarte de amendoa* (a tart made with ground almonds), *arroz doce* (a creamy rice pudding), *sonhos* (apricot fritters) and the quaintly named *toucinho do Céu*, literally 'salt pork from heaven', but in fact a confection made from beaten egg yolks and grated almonds.

The frequent use of almonds dates back to the Moors, who introduced almond trees to Portugal and Spain and planted wide groves in the Algarve, so that in spring, as their poets tell us, the landscape seemed covered with snow. After the Reconquest, the confection of the sweetmeats made by the Moors from egg-yolks and almonds, was taken up by the nuns in their convents, who later used chocolate as well. These little *bons bouches* and cakes are still extremely popular in Portugal, either at the end of a meal or around mid-afternoon, when the white-smocked school-children take advantage of the break to throng the *pastelarias*. In Viseu alone, the different varieties include: *Castanhas*, *Papos de Anjo*, *Ouriços*, *Pinguos de Tocha*, *Príncipes*, *Fios*, *Celeste* and *Tâmaras*.

Another pleasant way to end a meal is with the fresh fruit in season—figs, melons, medlars and cherries of a size and juiciness rarely encountered. The oranges, too, of which there are two crops a year, are splendidly sweet and juicy—and do *not* require the sugar with which the waiters are so prompt to heap them!

Cheese and charcuterie

Portuguese cheeses are not numerous and are mostly made from ewe's milk. One of the best is *Queijo da Serra* from the mountain massif of the Serra da Estrela, dividing the wide plains of the Alentejo from the Beira Alta and the wine-growing district of the Dão. It is a semi-hard cheese, but at its best has a creamy consistency and an entirely distinctive bite and flavour. *Queijo do Alentejo* is very similar, and there are small and delicious cream

169

cheeses from Azeitão in the Setúbal Peninsula, also made from ewe's milk and often served as an appetizer.

Hams, smoked or plain, and a variety of cured and spiced sausages are a speciality of the country. There is very little to choose between the Portuguese *presunto* and *chouriço* and the Spanish *jamón serrano* and *chorizos*, highly cured hams like those of Parma and Bayonne and spicy pepper sausages. The Portuguese maintain that the best of both are those from Lamego and Chaves in the north, which have a sweetness derived from the chestnuts on which the pigs were formerly fed; but unfortunately this is a practice which is dying out.

Other varieties of charcuterie, such as *morcela* (a black blood sausage) must be cooked, but *presunto* and *chouriço* are served as *hors d'oeuvres* and are also, with the fresh, crusty bread and a bottle of the local red wine, the makings of a good picnic. I have, in fact, in hotels where the cooking was uninspired, dined off thinly-shaved *presunto* and *Queijo da Serra*—and surprisingly well they went with an old 'Barca Velha'.

APPENDIX 1

Production of Portuguese Table Wines
1974, 1978 and 1980

Region	Production (hectolitres)		
	1974	1978	1980
Vinhos Verdes	2,964,368	1,728,422	1,568,842
Upper Douro	1,469,533	870,471	1,315,172
Dão	547,002	195,406	361,367
Moscatel de Setúbal	416,944	253,909	373,390
Colares	3,691	683	2,009
Bucelas	8,749	2,987	4,768
Carcavelos	396	225	267
Bairrada			489,557
Wines from J.N.V. areas	8,118,492	3,309,859	5,916,840
TOTAL	13,872,545	6,361,962	10,032,212

Note 1 The years 1974 and 1978 have been chosen as representative of maximum and minimum production over the recent period.

2 The figures for Moscatel de Setúbal include red table wines made within the demarcated area.

3 The Bairrada was not demarcated until 1979, so that its production in 1974 and 1978 is included in that of the areas administered by the Junta Nacional do Vinho.

APPENDIX 2

Exports of Bottled Wine and Wine Products from Portugal (litres)

	1978	1979	1980
Rosé wine	48,844,130	42,678,474	40,977,219
White wine	5,808,183	6,015,122	6,858,284
Red wine	2,871,607	3,174,339	5,010,131
Fortified wine (excluding Port and Madeira)	28,880	44,518	31,937
Vinegar	389,580	432,216	694,195
Sparkling wines	168,033	568,455	220,210
Vermouth	317,576	519,273	397,352
Brandy	812,342	1,121,465	1,207,835
Bagaceira	162,630	194,198	249,753
Red *vinho verde*	820,821	981,920	678,622
White *vinho verde*	3,502,870	4,130,877	4,182,209
Red Dão	1,223,559	1,379,651	1,465,098
White Dão	353,667	388,948	376,848
Moscatel de Setúbal	9,342	12,335	17,424
Red Colares	2,030	8,080	8,972
White Colares	248	660	2,116
Carcavelos	—	90	—
White Bucelas	14,111	33,297	21,060
TOTAL	65,329,609	61,683,918	62,399,537

APPENDIX 3

Exports of Port: Volumes and Value

Year	Volume (hl)			Total value (1000 escudos)
	In containers	In cask	Bottled	
1971	196,591	120,616	50,964	666,452
1972	245,371	116,989	72,586	882,421
1973	282,551	92,649	100,707	1,274,141
1974	286,929	45,771	104,386	1,881,501
1975	254,510	27,444	97,538	1,542,971
1976	238,966	18,873	153,128	1,719,427
1977	292,986	15,728	177,234	2,537,267
1978	274,389	12,985	233,679	3,756,250
1979	291,237	12,782	324,671	5,860,508
1980	270,780	10,705	333,017	7,217,633

Note These figures illustrate changing patterns in the export of Port and the growing trend towards shipments in container and bottle, rather than in cask.

Glossary of Portuguese and Technical Terms

ADEGA a cellar or winery.

AGARDENTE DE BAGACEIRA, *see* BAGACEIRA.

AGUARDENTE DE VINHO, AGUARDENTE brandy.

ANO year, used of a vintage, e.g. Ano 1973.

ARAME the fine wire mesh sometimes used on bottles of old *reservas*.

ARJOADO a system of training vines on wires stretched between trees.

ARMAZEM a warehouse or wine store.

ASSOCIADO a partner in a cooperative winery.

AUTOVINIFICADOR an automatic vinification vat allowing for continuous submersion of the 'cap'.

BAGA the elderberry juice of ill-repute, once used to colour Port.

BAGACEIRA *marc*, made by distilling BAGAÇO.

BALSEIRO a large wooden vat on legs.

BARCO RABELO an old-fashioned sailing ship used for transporting new wine from the Upper Douro to the Lodges in Vila Nova de Gaia across the river from Oporto.

BARDO a system of training vines on wire stretched between wooden posts or granite pillars.

BEESWING fine flakes of mucilage from the grape sometimes found in nineteenth-century Ports.

BICA ABERTA fermentation *en blanc*, without the presence of stalks, skins or pips.

BRANCO white.

BRUTO French *brut*, used to describe a very dry sparkling wine.

CADASTRO a register of vineyards.

CARVALHO oak.

CASTA a variety of grape.

CAVA *literally* a cellar, but often used to describe an establishment making sparkling wine by the Champagne method.

CEPA a vine.

CONCURSO NACIONAL the national competition for bottled wines organized annually by the Junta Nacional do Vinho.

CRUZETA a system of training vines on wires running between crosspieces attached to upright pillars.

CUBA DE FERMETAÇÃO   a vat for fermenting wine.

DEPOSITO   a large tank or vat for storing or blending wine.

DESENGAGE   the removal of stalks from the grapes.

DOCE   sweet.

ENGARRAFADO   bottled.

ESMAGAMENTO   the crushing of the grapes.

ESTALAGEM   a small country inn or hotel.

ESTUFA   a heated tank for maturing Madeira.

GARRAFA   a bottle.

GARRAFEIRA   *see* VINHO.

GEROPIGA   a sweet syrup made by evaporating down must.

GREEN WINES   *see* VINHO VERDE.

GREMIO   from the Latin *gremium*, a bosom; used to describe the two largest instruments of official control: the Junta Nacional do Vinho and the Instituto do Vinho do Oporto.

HOGSHEAD   a barrel equivalent to half a pipe and containing 160 litres.

LAGAR   an old-fashioned stone trough used for treading the grapes.

LEVADA   a narrow channel used in Madeira for irrigation.

LODGE   one of the large cellars in Vila Nova de Gaia, opposite Oporto, where Port is matured and blended.

LOTE   a parcel of new Port, subsequently to be matured and blended.

MACACO   a wooden paddle used in wine-making for submerging the *manta* or 'cap'.

MANTA   the 'cap', composed of grapeskins and other solid matter, which rises to the surface of the vat when making red wine.

MOSTO AMUADO   an evaporated must used for sweetening wine.

PIPE   the casks used in the Port lodges for maturing or shipping wines and of five types: lodge lot casks of about 630 litres, Douro casks of 550 litres, shipping pipes of 534·24 litres, hogsheads of 267 litres and quarter casks of 134 litres.

POIO   a terrace.

PORTO   the Portuguese name for Oporto.

POUSADA   a government-run hotel often sited in a historic building.

QUINTA   a country property, sometimes a chateau, sometimes a shed, the point being that it must embrace agricultural land.

SECO   dry.

SELO DE ORIGEM   the seal of origin guaranteeing the authenticity of a demarcated wine.

TAREFA DE BARRO   a large earthenware container used for fermenting wine.

TONEL pl. TONEIS   a large cask holding 13–25 pipes.

TRASFEGA   racking or decantation of the wine from the lees.

UVEIRA   a tree vine.

VELHO   old.

VERMUT   vermouth.

VINHO   wine.

APERITIVO   apéritif wine.

BRANCO   white wine.

CLARETE   light red wine.

CLARO   new wine.

CONSUMO   ordinary wine, *vin ordinaire*.

DE MESA   table wine.

176

VINHO   wine—cont.

ENGARRAFADO   bottled wine.

ESPUMANTE   sparkling wine.

ESTUFADO   'baked' wine, used of the process employed in Madeira for maturing it by heat.

GARRAFEIRA   a selected vintage with long bottle age.

GENEROSO   an apéritif or dessert wine rich in alcohol.

LICOROSO   a wine high in alcohol.

MADURO   a normal, mature table wine—as opposed to a *vinho verde.*

RESERVA   old wine of a good year.

ROSADO   rosé wine.

QINADO   a tonic wine containing quinine.

TINTO   red wine.

VERDE   a young wine, either white or red, which has undergone a special malolactic fermentation and evolved a slight sparkle.

Bibliography

Adega Regional de Colares, *O vinho de Colares*, Colares, 1938

Allen, H. Warner, *Sherry and Port*, London, 1952; *Good Wine from Portugal*, revised ed., London, 1952

Bradford, Sarah, *The Englishman's Wine—The Story of Port*, London, 1969

Carvalho, Bento de, and Correira, Lopes, *Os vinhos de nossa pais* (English trans. *The Wines of Portugal*, Junta Nacional do Vinho, Lisbon, 1979)

Cobb, Gerald, *Oporto Old and New*, privately printed 1966.

Cockburn, Ernest, *Port Wine and Oporto*, n.d.

Comissão de Viticultura da Região dos Vinhos Verdes, *Estudos*, Nos. 5 & 7, Oporto, 1962, 1971

Costa, B. C. Cincinnato da, *O Portugal vinícola* (*Le Portugal vinicole*), Lisbon, 1900

Croft, John, *A treatise on the Wines of Portugal*, 1788 (ed. Instituto do Vinho do Porto), Oporto, 1940

Croft-Cooke, Rupert, *Port*, London, 1957; *Madeira*, London, 1961

Delaforce, John, *The Factory House at Oporto*, Christie's Wine Publications, London, 1979

Exposição Internacional de 1874, *Breve noticia da viticultura portuguesa*, Lisbon, 1874

Federação dos Vinicultores do Dão, *Relatório e contas*, Viseu (statistics published annually)

Ferreira, J. A. Pinto, *O comercio do Vinho do Porto através da correspondencia de John Whitehead, Consul Britanico na mesma cidade, enderecada a Mr. Warre (1793 a 1800)*, Oporto, n.d.

Fletcher, Wyndham, *Port: An Introduction to its History and Delights*, London, 1978

Fonseca, Alvaro Moreira da, *O ABC da vinificão*, Oporto, 1960

Forrester, J. J., *The Oliveira Prize-Essay on Portugal*, London, 1853

Franco, António Porto Soares, *O Moscatel de Setúbal*, União Vinícola Regional do Moscatel de Setúbal, Lisbon, 1938

Galhano, Amândio Barbedo, *Le Vin 'Verde'*, Comissão de Viticultura da Região dos Vinhos Verdes, Oporto, 1951

179

Instituto do Vinho do Porto, *Regulations Governing the Description of Special Types of Port Wine (Vinho do Porto)*, Oporto, 1978; *O Vinho do Porto em 1980* (export statistics), Oporto, 1980

Journadas vitivinícolas da Bairrada (symposium on Bairrada wines held on 25–8 October 1979)

Loureiro, Virgilio Correira de, *La region délimitée des vins du 'Dão'*, Viseu, 1949

Manjón, Maite, *The Home Book of Portuguese Cookery*, London, 1974

Ministeries of Agriculture and Fisheries and of Trade and Tourism, *Ministerial Order No. 421/79 of 11th August, 1979* (defining the 'determinate areas')

Pereira, Gonçalves, *Les vignobles du Portugal, étude géographique*, Toulouse, 1932

Postgate, Raymond, *Portuguese Wine*, London, 1969

Read, Jan, *The Wines of Spain and Portugal*, London, 1973; *Guide to the Wines of Spain and Portugal*, London, 1977; *The Table Wines of Spain and Portugal*, in *André Simon's Wines of the World*, 2nd edn., London, 1981

Robertson, George, *Port*, London, 1979

Sandeman Sons & Co. Ltd., George G., *The House of Sandeman*, 4th edn., London, 1979

Simon, André, *Port*, London, 1934

Stanislawski, Dan, *Landscapes of Bacchus*, University of Texas Press, Austin, 1970

Vizetelly, Henry, *Facts about Port and Madeira*, London, 1880

Miscellaneous

Allen, H. Warner, *A History of Wine*, London, 1962

Cheke, Marcus, *Dictator of Portugal, A Life of the Marquis of Pombal*, London, 1938

Jeffs, Julian, *The Wines of Europe*, London, 1971

Johnson, Hugh, *The World Atlas of Wine*, 2nd ed., London, 1977; *Hugh Johnson's Pocket Wine Book*, London, 1981

Livermore, H. V., *A New History of Portugal*, Cambridge, 1966

Lord, Tony, *The World Guide to Spirits*, London, 1979

Michelin *Green Guide to Portugal*, London, 1980

Price, Pamela Vandyke, *A Directory of Wines and Spirits*, London, 1979

Redding, Cyrus, *A History and Description of Modern Wines*, 3rd edn., London, 1851

Schneider, Steven J., *The International Album of Wine*, New York, 1977

Sutcliffe, Serena, ed., *André Simon's Wines of the World*, 2nd edn., London, 1981

Symington, J. D., *Portugal, The Ancient Alliance*, London, 1960

Vizetelly, Henry, *The Wines of the World Characterized and Classed*, London, 1875

Index

Page numbers in italic refer to illustrations

geropiga, 41
glycerine, 103, 109
Gomes de Oliveira, Joaquim, 71
Graham, W. J. & Co., 39
Grant, William, 57
Grão Vasco (painter), 98
'Grão Vasco' (wine), 98, 107,
    109, 111, 112
grape varieties, *see* vine varieties
Greeks, 19
'green wines', *see vinhos verdes*
Gremio dos Exportadores do
    Vinho do Porto, 31
Guedella, Philip, 57
Guedes, D. Antonio van-Zeller,
    84
Guedes, D. Fernando van-Zeller,
    146
Guerra, D. João Pedro Miller, 88

Hal, Bluff King, 55
Hancock, Captain, 56
Harvey & Sons Ltd, John, 54, 63
Henry II, King of Castile, 20
Henry the Navigator, Prince, 21,
    38, 55, 168
'His Eminence's Choice' (port),
    52
Hood, Thomas, 65
Hunt, Roope & Co., 39
hybrids, 58

Instituto do Vinho do Porto, 31,
    51, 168
Insua, Quinta da, 107

Jeffs, Julian, 61
João II, King of Portugal, 30
Johnson, Hugh, 122
Junta Nacional do Vinho (JNV),
    31–3, 65

Kopke & Co. Ltd, 39
Kopke, Christian, 39

Koran, 20

labels, Portuguese, 36
labelling regulations, EEC, 34–5;
    UK, 36
Lafões, wines of, 127–8
lagares, 23, 29, 48, 49, 125
'Lagosta' (wine), 95
Lamego, 39, 153, 154
'Lancers' (wine), 26, 146, 149,
    150–1
'Lancers vinho verde' (wine), 88
late bottled vintage Port, 52
Leacock, John, 56
levadas, 58
Lima, 78, 95
Lodges, Port, 50–1
London International Exhibition
    of 1874, 24
Lorvão, Monastery of, 20, 114
lote, 50
Lusitanians, 19

macaco, 48, 70
Machado, D. Luís, 111
Madeira, 24, 31, 36, 55–63;
    history, 55–7; soils, grapes
    and elaboration, 58–60;
    types of Madeira, 60–1;
    exports and shippers, 62–3,
    71
Madeira cake, 60
Madeira Wine Association, 62
'Magrico' (wine), 96
Malmsey (wine), 59, 60, 61, 62
Mangualde, 99, 105; Cooperative
    of, 105
manta, 48
'Mateus' (wine), 26, 146, 147,
    150
Meão, Quinta de, 42, 48, 124–5,
    124
'Meia Encosta' (wine), 112
'Messias' (wine), 96